The
Lehi Key

THE
LEHI KEY

By Kelly Child

The Finisher's Publishing
Sonoma Co., California
2015

©2015 First Edition (Black & White)
The Finisher's Publishing
Sonoma Co., California
thelehikey@finisherspublishing.com

Edited by: Eric Thatcher
Contributing Editor: Mark Whitley
Front and Back Cover Design: Rob Thomas
Front cover photo: Jeff Saward

ISBN(10): 0692387021
ISBN(13): 978-0692387023

This book is dedicated to Wendi and our four wonderful children.

Contents

Contents

List of Figures, Photography & Illustrations

List of Figures, Photography & Illustrations

Introduction–A Great Clay Pot

A clay pot may be broken and its pieces scattered abroad over hills, in sundry climates, on the mountain tops and lost in wooded forests. Each of us in our journey through life gathers sets of experiences and observations that are ours alone. From beneath both the dusty path through desolation, that at times we may have had to walk, and from under the watery rocks of rivers waded in the summers of our soul, a voice speaks to us. If we give room to the words and let them take form in the gardens of our heart and mind, we gain imagery of the small piece of that broken clay pot that is ours to carry, behold and learn from. At times we may feel inspired to share with others and at other times we find it wise to refrain. Eventually we realize our piece truly is like no other, and that the piece that belongs to another is never entirely in its specificity just like ours. I believe if we could all clearly reveal each of our own pieces with lucid resolution to one another as we gather around the great campfire of an eternal family reunion, we might gain a glimpse of the Great Clay Pot in its wholeness and unity. Maybe we would see that it holds within it all truth and that from it issues forth the waters of life. What I am sharing in this book is the small piece that I've found. I'm pretty sure it's legitimately clay pot material. However, being that it has been extracted from rivers of time, as I waded through them, it is apparent that my piece is somewhat covered in green moss.

It was on a cold, damp, wintery afternoon in the wooded misty hills of Montebello Mountain about 6 years ago that I lamented my woes to Divinity in the heavens above and in the earth below. I was in the company of groves of old oaks and some of my sentiment went to their gnarled stumps and twisted branches; perhaps they'd relate. They too were covered in part with green moss. The paths along the hillsides were of firmly packed mud and the air was uniformly still. As I walked the winding path that traversed the northern face of the hill, I emerged from the woodland groves facing eastward; towards the esteemed valley of silicon. Between two of the more prominent hills in the east, a full moon was rising in the purple early evening sky. The fallen tree branches, rocks and trailside plants were alive together while a moist chill late winter's air kept those akin to comfort at home and not passing through these woods, leaving an immensity of space for the faintest of sounds to be heard; even a drop of dew falling from a leaf to a puddle below might be noticed. And so as soon as I could get a pen in hand I wrote the poem that the scene inspired.

"A Spring Poem"

The Earth is my favorite book; her loyal pages tell no lies. Truth springs from her soil. No man can put his spin on her; no reporter, no politician, for she only dances on her axis with her Lover, her Dance partner, the Sun.

His arms turn her gracefully in the royal courtyard, taking her by the hand to turn her in time, as upon a swirl in a mighty river of virtue flowing from his shoulder.

And with swords of truth at the hilt, Sentinels of stone stand guard, placed there by Heavenly parents, who are the Eternal Authors of the Universe.

And though the Sun must be set, the full moon rises in the East to turn the page, and my soul is at rest. She reads to me.

Spring is my favorite season, at this time of the year.
The winter is passed. The full moon rose in her coronation between two great mountains to watch over the night; her reflection cast upon the lake.

She took yesterdays' chapter and the truth that she gave me with her. It was more than I could bear.
Though I desired to stay awake and stand guard, I fell through the mists into slumber. And my soul received rest.

And in the morning of spring, outside my window, a bird sings the song of the season, a scent of a rose, though but a wisp in the breeze is my guide.

And Virtue's Knowledge as the dews of heaven also rest on their petals, where did the mists of night go? Where is their power?

And in a fourth there is a third, the number of my favorite song; the East morn Sun beams cut through in two, and in the light there is no wrong.

From the lake his sword is returned, the Master to His waiting bone, the coronation of her King returned, to take his rightful throne. Spring has returned! The bees and creatures are voicing, the King and Queen provide the feast and wine, a great day for rejoicing!

But where is the page of yesterday's chapter, who read and wrote of the lovers' dance, placed under guard by some stone sentinel in the East, the meridians of Velocity, Probability and Chance? But never mind that book is lost, the pages taken back, the Spring is here, the Sun has returned, I can't think of one thing that I lack.

The Earth, Moon and Stars are now my favorite pages, a new book in the Sun's light; the rivers, mountains, breezes and sun are always sure and right.

I read in awe.

Part I

Le Mystère de Cathèdrale de Chartres

The Train to Chartres

The year is 2010. The location is France. Having severely injured my right wrist on a coin operated punching bag game in Liverpool with an English coworker a week earlier, I tarried forth through the countryside of France by train. And so it is that the mystery ensues. I carried with me a red book. On the cover of the red book is a mangy grey bird with a green snake in its beak resting upon a crown above a shield of red. A white chevron spans the shield and is the background for 7 fleur de lys symbols. Inside is a history and genealogy of the Long Haired Kings of Gaul; pagan kings rumored to have never cut their hair, as their power flowed from its lengths. Victors over Attila, they delivered justice to the plundering Huns. Their mythos is unprecedented, yet their posterity did humble themselves after their tragic fall. As the train moved swiftly through the French countryside, I looked out the window towards the Northeast of the train, since I was sitting in the backwards seat as we travelled from Paris to Chartres. The rolling hills were wooded and grassy. I saw from my window a great stone wall that seemed to divide a ravine. The grey stone held the cold of the morning as the rays of the sun traced their geometry through the blue winter sky. The sharpened longswords of light rays divided the aether in twain and seemed to promise warmth. I didn't notice any streams that might be good for fly fishing for trout. The train slowed down as we approached the station in the small town of Chartres. I worked to fit the red book back into my overstuffed daypack, which was weighted down with books, train maps and an excess of English pounds, Euro coins, chewing gum, bottled water and normal travel stuff. My travel buddy, Greg, met up with me as we got off of the train. It was chilly and crisp outside, but reasonable for February. The plane tickets are much more affordable in the off-season. Anyway, Greg is an old fly fishing buddy. He and I have fished many of the best creeks in the west. His father and my grandfather worked at Lockheed Martin during the cold war era. Greg had never been to Europe and was a willing and courageous travel partner. What I mean by courageous is that working those train-ticket machines can humble, bewilder and frustrate an American engineering-minded man. To increase the intensity of the adventure, at one point Greg had walked through the train station's automated security gate contraption and the gate arms closed swiftly before he had managed to pull his suitcase through, separating the two. It was pretty funny. As I recall, he had to go back through, purchase another ticket and go through the gate again; this time successfully getting both himself and his luggage through.

So, what makes for a good European adventure is to bring along a few good questions. The question deeply and securely held in my heart was vague but had to do with the number 14. Yes, many come to France for cheese and wine and I was here regarding the number 14. You see 14 thrice itself is mysterious. And in Chartres, France there is a cathedral dedicated in the year 1260 A.D. (14 x 3 x 30) And in that cathedral is a stone labyrinth built into the flooring that according to English Prince Nicholas De Vere is 14 x 3 feet in diameter. This is significant to De Vere as he relates that the sum of the digits of the Roman measure of the Jerusalem Mile of 1760 yards = 14 and when multiplied by the number of feet in a yard he arrives at the expression 14 x 3 = 42. The labyrinth is only symbolically suggestive of the Jerusalem mile, and not literally that length.[1] It has indeed been measured to have an average diameter of 42 ft. 3 and 2/3 inches according to labyrinth specialist Jeff Saward.[2] Meanwhile, author M. Garfield Cook makes the astounding yet apparently unrelated observation that "14 x 3 = 42" is observed in the grouping of the genealogical generations from Abraham to Jesus Christ in the Joseph Smith translation of The Book of Matthew.[3] [4] Joseph Smith groups the generations in 3 verses of 14 generations each for a total of 42 generations. 42 generations x 30 years/generation = 1260 years, which is the year the Chartres Cathedral is dedicated with labyrinth in place. To make matters more engaging yet, in The Book of Revelations, John sees that "the woman fled into the wilderness where she hath a place prepared of God, that they should feed her there a thousand two hundred and threescore days". But Joseph Smith corrects that verse to read 1260 "years" rather than "days". What is the connection between these expressions and what can I learn by visiting the labyrinth in Chartres Cathedral?

Unlike standing in lines for a crepe in Paris, my train ride to Chartres seemed epic. Now, if someone had ordered 42 crepes in 3 groups of 14, I might have taken a closer look at crepes in Paris, but I didn't notice anyone do that.

So after Greg and I left from the train station we walked up the large hill that the town center stood upon. It seemed like a good strategic location to build a town based on my limited

---

[1] DeVere, Nicholas, "The Dragon Legacy", 2004, The Book Tree Publishing, p. 136.

[2] Saward, Jeff, 2014, www.labyrinthos.com

[3] Joseph Smith's "New Translation" of the Bible, Herald Publishing House, 1970.

[4] Cook, M.Garfield, "Cornerstones of the Restoration, A Message Extracted From a Genealogical Record", 1998.

knowledge of medieval history. The town was everything an American tourist would hope a small town in the venerated French countryside should be. As we followed our directions we finally saw the tall steeples crisply standing in the distance. Eventually we arrived facing the front entrance to the Cathedral, which faces eastward and thusly we were facing west.

At this point I'd like to point out that upon entering a new contemplation of the mysteries, there is often an accompanying question posed to the initiate regarding the preparedness of his or her heart and intentions. I would mention that over the door at the entrance to Plato's school there was a sign that stated, "Let No Man Ignorant of Geometry Enter". If you've ever attempted taking a math class without having successfully taken the proper prerequisites, you know what a terrible experience that can be. Though, if you have studied the proper prerequisites you may have a great experience in learning something new that is built on the foundation of the previous material. The Lord teaches us directly "precept upon precept, line upon line".[5] "For the day of the Lord is great and very terrible and who can abide it?"[6]

In 1891 in Languedoc, France, a man by the name of Francois Berenger Sauniere placed a sign over the door to the church that he took care of called Rennes Le Chateau. The sign read, "This place is terrible".[7] So I guess that might mean, "This place is great". And if we dig deeper into the crypts of time hearkening back to Egypt to the Hor Book of Breathings of Isis papyrus, which found way with expediency to Joseph Smith Jr.,

---

[5] Isaiah 28:10

[6] Joel 2:11

[7] Twyman, Tracy R. "Merovingian Mythos and the Mystery of Rennes le Chateau", 2004, Dragon Key Press, p.8.

we may read: "Come Osiris Hor, justified, born of Taykhebyt, justified. May you enter the Hall of the Two Truths, having been purified from every sin and misdeed. Stone of Truth is your name."[8] So, let's go into the cathedral at Chartres and take a look around.

[8] Rhodes, Michael D., "Hor Book of Breathings: A Translation and Commentary", 2002, The Foundation for Ancient Research and Mormon Studies, p. 29.

The Thresh of Chartres Cathedral

I. Abraham and his son Isaac stand upon the shoulders of the sacrificial ram;
depicted in the second statue to the right.

We walked the perimeter of the cathedral before entering. So many of the statue characters carved in the niches appeared to be of normal men, women, common people, common beasts and common day activities. My favorite was a curled up sleeping dog. Some bit of time after my visit to the cathedral I learned that Pythagoras and Aristotle were found in humble positions carved in their own niches. The general message of the statues seems to be that all of God's children stand upon the shoulders of the hard work and sacrifice of those who have humbly gone on before us. Pythagoras is depicted as a simple man anxiously engaged in writing. Above him is a woman with a harp ringing a bell. His studies and contemplations led to a better understanding of musical vibration and of geometry and are still the basis of what we understand about the octave. The West side of the cathedral is built with flying buttresses that appear to be great grey stone cogs and gears extending to engage with the sky above. The round stained glass windows all around the cathedral appear to be gears within gears, turning the heavens above and the hands of time below. From within, the great windows tell stories from the Bible and illuminate both the cathedral and the visitor. The stone carvings below reflect the messages in the windows above and combine to tell the full story.

The cathedral location had been a place of spiritual pilgrimage from the times of the Merovingian and Carolingian Dynasties and even back to the times of the Druids. A cathedral seems to have existed there for centuries. Its more famed early architect, Fulbert, had come to Chartres from the Rheims Cathedral School in 990 A.D. This was 4 years after the passing of Lothair King of the West Franks. Meanwhile the descendants of the Merovingian dynasty were slowly being scattered as they descended from political involvement into the wilderness of the common man and more importantly to a new found freedom. The scattering was marked by the dethroning and tonsuring of Childeric III by Pepin the Short in 751 A.D. This ended a sad era where generations of Merovingian boy-kings had literally been held hostage by a secret combination of Ripuarian Franks for 113 years. The Mayors of Neustria held captive the male bloodline for their own political purposes and then would kill the boy-kings before they were beyond their mid 20's in age.

The release of the family from political bondage gave them a new freedom to pursue sovereignty in their own families with no interest in returning to the throne. However their focus on spiritual matters was highly sustained in Southern France and their name held enough prestige and their prosperity extended

II. The front of Chartres cathedral faces northeast.

well enough into the next generations that they had means to be of no small effect. Their dedication in service of Jesus and Mary Magdalene would have an auspicious influence that would come to light many, many generations later and later bless their posterity. Of the various branches of the families of the House of Merovech, the family of Childegaire played a special roll in caring for the church of Jesus and Mary Magdalene. The various family members served as seigneurs of several castles in Corbigny and Vezelay. During the 9th century members of the Childegaire family helped establish several monasteries dedicated to Jesus and Mary Magdalene. Vezelay would become the primary meeting center for those that venerated Mary Magdalene. Charles the Bald, who was a descendent of Pepin the Short, is rumored to have donated a garment that belonged to Mary Magdalene known as the Sancta Camisia to the early Cathedral in Chartres in 876 A.D., the exact same year that Childebert I, descendent of Childeric III, took oath to become the fidelis of King Charles the Bald. Thusly the descendant families of Pepin the Short and Childeric III had a spirit of kinship. Childegaire IV died in 990 A.D. as Bishop of Limoges. His son Alwin stepped into his position and the continuation of the Merovingian support for Cluniac monasticism supported a good era of increase in knowledge, spiritual and cultural prosperity. Cluny II Abbey was built from 954 -981 A.D. and would become the largest library in France. It was built in Romanesque style. In contrast, the cathedral in Chartres would become the first of a new architectural style in Europe, the gothic cathedral.

The cathedral was not just a place of religious worship but also a university of education. Fulbert's successors were Ivo of Chartres (1040-1117 A.D.) and Bernard of Chartres (1119-1124 A.D.). Bernard's younger brother had compiled a

Heptateuchon, which was an encyclopedia of the Seven Liberal Arts. The mind was believed to be enlightened through the study of the Quadrivium, which consisted of arithmetic, geometry, astronomy and music. The Trivium consisted of three parts: grammar, logic and rhetoric. Elements of these seven disciplines are found in the stonework of the cathedral. The Cathedral was destroyed by a fire in 1194 A.D. and later rebuilt and rededicated. The crypts however remained preserved. Inside the cathedral a labyrinth is inlaid in the stone floor. Pilgrims to the cathedral walk its path under the light of the west rose stained glass window. The path of the labyrinth is known to some as the Jerusalem mile.

The First Arch

"...Yea having had a great knowledge of the goodness and mysteries of
God, therefore I make a record of my proceedings in my days"

- Nephi (1 Nephi 1:1)

As we walked through the entry into the cathedral from the
North porch, all of my senses were engaged. I come from
California. We don't have old things unless they are still part of
nature like the redwood trees or the giant stone megaliths in
Yosemite Valley that were carved out by glaciers in the last ice
age. Our artisanship is found in the sub-micron etchings in
silicon used to compute inconceivable amounts of information or
in the transfer of that information through the use of light in an
internet of collective thought, order and consciousness. Our
intellect is encoded in software that may be understood in an
abstract form of architecture, but deeply underlying the code at
the foundation are binary and hexadecimal numeric counting
systems and numbers that form information that then represents
thought. These codes are typically kept safe behind login
passwords and cryptographic tokens. Yet here from another time
stand before me the technologies of 1,000 years ago. Those
whose hands worked with the hammer and chisel, with the
square and with compass, with sweat and with toil built a
standing record in stone. They reached for the stars and carved
their story in rock hewn from the earth. What may be found in
their numbers and geometries? As I looked all around it was

clear that the aptitude of the engineers of 1000 years ago was on par with today's best engineers, though they lived in a time few of us really have the time or means to understand. While standing in the north I saw a couple of men with measuring tapes measuring the lengths between pillars. I stayed silent to hear the echoes reverberate through the canopies of chiseled stone. I walked to the westernmost part of the cathedral below the large stained glass Rose window and began to slowly walk east. I brought with me my little black journal to record impressions.

The cathedral's floor plan when viewed from above looks similar to a cross. The central lower portion is called the nave. The arms of the cross are called the transepts and the upper portion is called the choir. The Chartres cathedral is oriented with the choir and front of the cathedral facing slightly East of North East. The nave in Chartres cathedral contains seven arches on either side defined by eight tall pillars. Unlike much architecture, these arches have no dropping keystone but rather meet at the apex to appear as the intersection of two circles. After the seven arches the eighth arch in its expansive reach spans the North and South transepts. 4 more arches thereafter lead towards the east choral area to what I now refer to as the 13th area, where Mary and Child are in the position of honor. This corresponds in floor plan orientation with the Lady Room in Roslyn Chapel in Edinburgh Scotland. And if we walk from West to East towards the 13th area to the Child Savior in Mother's Arms, whose luster is above that of the sun at noon day, we shall have passed with spiritual endowment, as it were, 12 others whose brightness did exceed that of the firmament.[1]

---

[1] Book of Mormon 1 Nephi 1: 8-10

The walk through the cathedral for me was an experiment of faith to listen to the message of the cathedral. So since the creative periods in the Book of Genesis are six with a seventh that is rest, I decided to reflect on what I could remember of Day 1 of the creation. Initially there is void. The void seems to slightly precede the events that follow. God says, "Let there be light". So, the number one is a representation of wholeness and unity. But void was wholeness as well. When God's voice permeated the Void and the Void begat light, those electromagnetic propagations were nurtured in a womb of void. The representation of void is not being seen in the stone of arch and pillar, but felt in the stillness that is impregnated with the humming small sounds that move through the Cathedral; the essence itself. And, so, in the creation sequence, God speaks saying there is both light and dark. All of creation that follows builds upon these opposite principles, as taught by Moses of Egypt. Metaphorically, these two states constitute the most fundamental pair of pillars of existence and are but a reflection of our Heavenly Parents.

In the generation preceding Pythagoras there lived a wise father in the Mediterranean area who had raised his sons with both Judaic tradition and learning, but also in Egyptian tradition. And so the small portion of teachings through him that were preserved reflect much Egyptian thought and the Egyptian mathematics of the time period of 600 B.C. His name is known as Lehi. In the accounts of his visions found in the Book of Mormon, he relates the heavens opening up to him. He saw two things. He saw God sitting on his throne with numberless concourses of angels surrounding him; and he also saw "One" (with a capital "O"). The One descended out of the midst of heaven and twelve others followed him. Lehi reveals no names associated with either the One or the twelve, however, he does describe the brightness of the One to be above that of the noon day sun and he describes the brightness of the twelve to be above the brightness of the stars in the firmament. His assignment of the symbol of stars to the "twelve others" seems to signify to the mind an imagery of twelve constellations. As we consider the twelve expansive arches that line the procession from the Royal Portal of the cathedral to the Virgin and Child, we can imagine the twelve constellations dropping to the night time horizon over the course of the year. While the One, in a sense, may seem separate like a separate figure, in fact, the work of the One is to unify the twelve; to make them "at one" or to atone.

The number one is a symbol of unity. It is also a symbol of wholeness. The whole Chartres Cathedral is unity, from the stonework architecture to the air that fills it, and from the waters of the sweat of workers under the stone, to the light illuminating the stained glass windows. It is all one piece of art. It is one body and all of its parts work together to create a living message. Geometric symbolism is important for us to understand in order to understand the cathedral; geometric symbolism is one of the languages the cathedral speaks. Because the number one is a symbol of origin, "One" may be represented geometrically as a single point. It is the point source from which light radiates. The sun is considered in light physics to be a perfect point source. Also, because 'One' is a numeric equivalent of 'All' of the parts of the whole, another good geometric symbol for One is the circle. It is complete, whole and perfectly round. The One and the twelve of Lehi's vision are symbols of Jesus and the twelve disciples. Let's solemnly consider that the One or the Lord may be represented as a single geometric point and that the twelve may be represented by the circle, denoting their wholeness as a body; perfect as a body, though certainly humanly imperfect and incomplete as individuals. With Christ as their center, they are complete and whole. Likewise, the Chartres Cathedral with Christ at its center is whole. Even more importantly is our stewardship; our body is a temple of God, our parts are distinct, our minds are broken and conflicted, we may incur wounds to our sensitive souls, the very material with which we are built is less than the dust of the earth in its parts. Yet somehow we have the composure to stand inside of great stone cathedrals, to walk, to think, to love and to act. When our heart is broken into meekness, we become contrite; we may then be made whole.

Lehi's vision of the twelve and the One descending from the midst of the heavens starts shortly after a pillar of fire came and dwelt on a rock before him. As far as we can tell from the account, the origin of the fire is not designated. We may envision air parting in twain, like as if air itself were a veil of firmament-cloth rent in twain to reveal something thinner. And so it was that through the tear in the air, Lehi, saw dwelling upon a rock the radiant flux of a flame of fire.

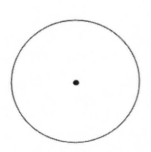

III. The Egyptian symbol for the Sun.

Fire has been considered in all times to be a source of life. The warmth inside of us is borrowed from the warmth endowed upon us by the flame of the sun. It is sunlight that the tree takes in through its leaves, yielding both oxygen and fruit, which sustain life. The air of the atmosphere, through which the pillar of fire that Lehi saw standing before him, also, is taken in by the leaves of the tree.

Fire and air, when considered in the classical body of elements, are considered to be the active elements. They are symbols of "things which act"[2] and they both feed the top part of the tree.

On his deathbed, Lehi imparted knowledge and reason to each of his sons saying, "And if there is no God we are not, neither the earth, for there could have been no creation of things, neither *to act* nor *to be acted upon*..."[3] So, let's walk on to discuss what comes to mind upon a consideration of the 2nd Arch.

---

[2] Book of Mormon, 2 Nephi 2:14

[3] Book of Mormon, 2 Nephi 2:11 (Hereafter the books within the Book of Mormon will only be cited and the words "Book of Mormon" will be omitted.)

The Second Arch

"For it must needs be that there is an opposition in all things..."
-Lehi (2 Nephi 2:11)

At the time I was in the cathedral, I had a sense of my own smallness. I noticed that there was a distinction between the arches here and the construction of the arches found in St. Clair cathedral in Roslyn. In the architecture of the small cathedral in Roslyn, one can find an angel placed at the meeting point of two arches located right at the joint above the supporting pillar. The wings of each angel extend to either side of the pillar. They sublimely seemed to suggest to the mind that the arch itself might be considered to be the expansive extension of the wings of an angel to either side of the pillar. According to the account by the early 1800's seer, Joseph Smith Jr., the wings of the beasts in the Book of Revelations represent *power* and the ability to move or *act*.[1] So, though the arches in the cathedral at Chartres featured no angels built in stone, yet I saw the great arches above to represent the power to move; a force of causation that the sun, moon and stars may give their light and roll upon their wings.[2] The wings of one arch span to intersect with the wings of the next. The angelic stone body to whom the wings report is the pillar between each arch. The stationary pillar carries the weight

---

[1] Doctrine and Covenants 77:4

[2] Doctrine and Covenants 88:45

and load put upon it. It is *acted upon* under the forces of gravity. Matter coupled with the force of gravity in free space yields acceleration. The necessity of opposition to maintain balance is the message of the second arch; light and dark, right and left, matter in an ordered state and matter in an unordered state or *prima materia*, cold and hot, wet and dry, North and South and so on.

A wound is often associated with initiation. The double sided axe or the two edged sword are symbols of division or a split. Where the wound occurs, things are divided in twain and where the wound is healing, atonement and the word are summoned.

In Mormon theology, before the Earth was created there was a pre-existence. When the councils of the gods regarding creation ensued, God's two great spirit-children found their leadership plans to be in opposition to each other. The laws with which Jesus and Lucifer grappled pertained to things that both act and are acted upon preceding the formation of the Earth. One proposed that the children of God come to earth and be given the agency to choose. This was Jehovah. Counsels were had with Heavenly Father or Elohim regarding the plan of creation and salvation. Things are being divided during this phase of creation. Yet as things are being divided, their potential for reunion and their connectivity at a distance yet remains. Consistent with the Egyptian concepts of the connection of all things, Lehi the sage, in his discussion with his sons also teaches that while there indeed is opposition in all things, "all things must needs be a compound in one". He then posits that all things are as one body. Honoring thy Father and Mother seems to exemplify that the natural law is for children to feel a unity with their parents. Similar to how children are begotten and are parts of their parents, in a universal sense all things are, as Lehi says, a compound in one or have a familial relationship. As the forces of gravity or the weak and strong electromagnetic forces may take upon themselves matter and so become dressed, so too Life may be dressed in matter. The great plan of our Heavenly Father included provisions that we should become more like him. For this reason as spiritual children of Heavenly Father and Mother, it was key in the plan to come down to Earth where our spirits would be clothed in temporal bodies of physical matter. In other words, we were born. Like Cinderella's shoe given to her of the prince, life takes on only that which fits. And thusly "all things" are dressed individually yet still a compound in one…at a distance. Because of this, seeking to become a law unto oneself is to no avail; we are bound under the same immoveable eternal laws.[3]

In the study of physics in modern universities, these principles are readily found, used and relied upon. A ray of light is born of a point source and its union with the parent point source is yet a familial one; because the two at a distance still may be expressed as a wave in harmony or of the same frequency as each other. If one Mass represented as M is divided into two smaller masses M_1 and M_2, there is a center of mass, M_3, which is equal to the sum of its parts M_1+M_2. No matter how many times the parent mass is divided, its children parts experience a force of attraction with the center of mass *continually relocating*. A vector or a line, which is commonly symbolized by the letter R, may represent this force coupled with a geometric direction; the royal **R**. R stands for radius. It also stands for rectitude. And

---

[3] Doctrine and Covenants 88:35 (Hereafter the Doctrine and Covenants will be abbreviated to "D&C".

so all of the physical parts are "at-one" at a distance, yet free to be acted upon by any force that may have *"power to act"*, as represented in the cathedral by arches and more particularly in the angelic stone wings. The principles may be auspiciously discovered precept upon precept, or at times precept under precept, in the movements of life clothed in their manifold wardrobes; and the royal throne begets unto life its seat in the material world.

The line segment as a unit of measure may also find kindred meaning with "the rod" in ancient scripture. The rod of iron is an important symbol of measure, law and attractive force as well.

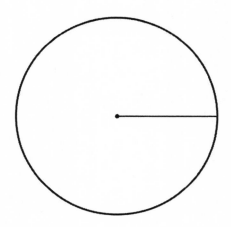

IV.   The line segment symbolizes the number 2, the
Word of God or the two-edged sword of truth.

V.   The radius inside the circle symbolizes the Lord circumscribing the bounds
of life into unity, yet dividing the circle within. The duality typifies the two-
sided nature of creation. The radius is the iron rod.

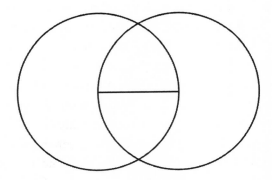

VI. Two interlaced circles with a common radius symbolizes reflection and opposition. Their cross section represents atonement; the arc angles imply spiritual action, velocity and acceleration and thusly classical potential energy.

An interesting property of iron is that when struck against a stone, it creates a spark. In a sense, fire is 'in the rod' and by smiting it against the stone, fire is being divided and extracted out from it. [Late 1700's English practitioner of arcane sciences, Francis Barrett, clarifies that "fire" is contained within the earth as well as in water.[4]] Modern physics would concur that energy is in all existing things as either kinetic or potential energy and any energy one way or other can be converted to heat or a spark and thusly fire under the right conditions.

The classical ancient elements, fire (sunlight) and air, feed the top parts of the tree. Sunlight and air are considered to be "things which act" or active principles. The bottom of the tree is

---

[4] Barrett, Francis, "The Magus, A Complete System of Occult Philosophy", 1801, p. 73-77.

nourished through its roots by water and the nutrients in the earthen soil. Water and earth as symbols are traditionally and generally considered to be things which are "acted upon".[5]

Overall, the principles extracted resulting from contemplation upon the second arch is that of division, opposition and duality. One axis of duality would be things which act and things which are acted upon. Another axis of duality would be masculine and feminine attributes. The "two pillars" is a very fundamental working symbolism as will be discussed in the discussion of the third arch. The account of the great creation by Moses in the book of Genesis clearly demonstrates the importance of division and duality in the creative process. Adam and Eve would also be faced with paradox, and they themselves are as the two great pillars and paradox of the human family.

While visiting Chartres Cathedral and walking from West to East through the nave, I felt eager anticipation to examine the stone labyrinth in the floor work, so let's move on to the third arch.

---

[5] 2 Nephi 2:13

The Third Arch

"And behold the third time they did understand the voice which they heard."
-Nephi (3 Nephi 11:6)

VII. The labyrinth floor plan was measured and provided by labyrinth specialist Jeff Saward.

When Greg and I had entered the Cathedral, I immediately had noticed that chairs were set up in preparation for a choral performance. Tourists buzzed around like bees over the stone labyrinth as they tried to take photos of the eye-catching grand views within the great cathedral. Walking the path of the labyrinth would be impossible. However, looking at the labyrinth and imagining the pilgrim's walk was not. And if the arches that held up the canopy of the cathedral above had "power to move", particularly in the imagination, then the arches in the labyrinth below may also have "power to move" written in their design.

The labyrinth is positioned with its center in the line defined by two pillars, transverse to the straight walk Eastward. These two pillars on the North and South sides separate the third and fourth arches. The labyrinth is sectioned in four quarters with its entrance at the West, as is the Royal Portal of the Cathedral itself. Its exit is the same path as the entrance, though upon exiting the tourist and spiritual pilgrim will now be coming from the East, headed West, which notably is in the same direction that the sun navigates the waters of the blue sky above each day.

I had once asked one of the many available Phil Campbells in the world why it seems that things get weird between three and four. Any story, tradition or ritual where there is a procession or rite of passage, things get a little perilous between three and four, to say the least. His response made sense to me. He said, "Imagine you are walking on a straight line through rational numbers, eventually you will get stuck at pi and can't get around it." The number that the symbol π represents is infinitely irrational. By nature, as a division, this ratio is a two-part conflict, and as Plato said, "The war never ends." Michael the archangel will have long-term employment. Successful passage from three to four requires that one lets go of two. In other words, one must let go of a rigid attachment to seeing the world in the duality of black and white. One must bid farewell to Kansas for the space of a time. In Japanese, the number four is considered unlucky as it is the number of death. The Kanji character for 4 shows legs inside a mouth, which indicates that someone is getting "consumed". No one ever knocks on the door exactly four times. In all of the various counting systems they use, the number four always goes irregular (usually shifting from "shi" to "yon").

As I stood there between the third and fourth pillars, the incommensurable irrationality seemed to me like the elephant in the room, or rather the Minotaur in the room. As one attempts to walk from West to East in a straight line, if all that were in between the Royal Portal before Arch 1 and the Christ Child and Virgin at space 13 were considered number, one would get irreconcilably stuck at 3.14. Looking around as you stand before the infinite abyss of pi before you, you would see you are stuck between the third and fourth arches. You might imagine walking into the cave of Pythagoras. One of his sentinels stops you abruptly with sword point brought to your breast. "Ouch! That's sharp!" The swords name is pi. Even the numeric value of pi has a 1 stuck right between a 3 and a 4 right after "the point" and that's the point. As far as technology goes, this gothic labyrinth as a stone-flooring monument accentuates the value that the simple symbol begotten of two pillars of opposition bears. The symbol is π. And π is a *transcendental* number. It also plugs up what would otherwise be a big belly button in the middle of the cathedral; an infinite abyss that tourists might fall into and the point of much contention. Because it is there and well built, both the faithful and profane walk right over it.

A consideration and contemplation upon the symbols of the labyrinth is a revealing adventure in thought. The circular pattern of the labyrinth declares maternal femininity and particularly the womb. After all, we are in the *nave*. The straight lines that appear as a cross and give structure to the labyrinth switchbacks define and separate four quarters of the labyrinth. The linearity of the cross betokens the qualities of masculinity within the femininity. Each line segment represents rectitude and summoning the earth, yet each line segment divides the labyrinth into its four quarters; as does the Quadrivium of Thierry and the four basic elements: fire, water, earth and air. (Though at some other level at the time I may have thought...tacos, hamburgers, burritos and a soda. It was getting to be near lunchtime...and I missed American food. But being acquainted with fasting, I subdued my levity, lest my thoughts be turned to a pillar of salt. Oh yeah, pillars...) To the South was a pillar and to the North was a Pillar. I didn't notice this at the time, but on the South wall beyond the South Aisle is a stained glass window depicting Adam and Eve in two scenes, the one above the other. In the scene above is a Tree with white fruit, in the scene below that one is a scene with a Tree with red fruit. We recall that Lehi taught that there must needs be opposition in all things and that an atonement must be made. Reflected below in the center of the stone labyrinth is what appears to be a tree symbol consisting of 6 smaller circles encircled in one greater circle. This is the centermost part of the labyrinth and is found halfway on the pilgrimage in to the center and out again. It is a place of contemplation. It is also known as a rose symbol. The 6 smaller circles almost define a Star of David symbol and all that it represents, however, with the space required for the opening, the geometry is slightly unsettled, unbalanced and so the Star of David symbol does not quite resolve. But then temporal nature tends to be like that. Trees themselves do not grow symmetrically. Imagine a walk through a forest where all the trees are perfectly balanced and symmetrical, no bends in the branches, no twists and no aged oaks. It would be lifeless. This slight imbalance and uneven ratio enables life. The pillar to the North and the Pillar to the South each have different symbolic meanings, the one representing male and the other female. The two pillars are equal in value, yet distinct in nature. And as things were divided in Day 1 and 2 as symbolized in Arch 1 and 2, masculine and feminine are divided yet attracted.

The labyrinth has a long history in human thought. Ancient spirals etched in rocks, caves and buildings denote the universally common contemplation of the spiral and all that it represents.

Pi is not alone in its mysterious place in the nature of number. Nay, phi also gives the world of labyrinth a twist. The spiral manifests itself everywhere from ancient Minoan art to the very wisps of torrential wind that lift Dorothy off on her adventure to discover Oz. Even the grand pigeon has seen the winds of storm before descending to find rest on dry ground.

An ancient clay disk found in a Minoan palace on the island of Crete called the Phaistos Disk dates back to 1700 B.C. It is round and on one side contains a spiral type labyrinth pattern with a flower in the center. The center flower has 7 petals. At varying intervals in partitions en route to the center of the spiral, there are smaller flowers that have 6 petals each. Counting the cross sections in a linear fashion across the diameter of the Phaistos Disk there are 3.5 segments from the edge to center of the spiral, or 7 across the entire horizontal diameter. Comparing this 3.5 factor to the Chartres Labyrinth switch backs, we find that there are 4 and 3 for an average of 3.5 per quadrant from the outer circumference to center. The central flower may be considered to be a *marigold*. In the case of the Phaistos Disk there are 19 internal segments, which may be taken to represent a period of time. It happens to be the case that there is a blue moon 7 times every 19 years.[1] 19 years is a Metonic cycle. So

---

[1] See Appendix A: The ratio of 19/7 is equivalent to the transcendental number *e* or 2.71.

again we are experiencing an observation upon the times and seasons of a cyclical process related to lunar cycles. Lunar cycles are in close proximity to feminine processes associated with fertility. The inner 19 segments are surrounded at the periphery of the disk by 11 segments. The ratio of the number of outer segments to the number of times the inner spiral crosses the diameter is 19 to 7; this ratio is 2.71 or the natural number *e*. There is a 12th piece that seems to be the key that holds the geometry together like a cork or keystone and suggests that the 12 segments represent the zodiac. This side of the disk has a general theme of circularity. The other side of the disk is riddled with what appears to be a geometers square and tells a different story. This would make sense that one side tends to the circular and the feminine and the other side tends to the square and the masculine. On the masculine side, the entrance to the labyrinth passes 4 small circles on the way in and the center is approximately a triangle of 3 sides. It seems that it was challenging for the creator of the disk to reconcile the three sides of the triangle geometrically with the circular swirls of the labyrinth since the lines end up being bent. You might say that's bending the rules. As we discussed earlier, many models and expressions have been developed to attempt to convey the same universal observations.

The Phaistos Disk and labyrinth at Chartres are two models of about the same thing, but may have a different emphasis. They attempt to describe and point the contemplator towards eternal truths. The disk motif and numeric symbols suggest that these also contained systems for measurement of astronomical events. In fact, the Chartres Labyrinth looks generally like the Antikythera Mechanism, which is a peculiar gear based contraption thought to have been built in the 1st century B.C.

The Antikythera Mechanism, to the best of modern knowledge, would have been exceptionally accurate in its ability to predict events or more practically said, measure time. Similar to the Chartres labyrinth, it is toothed with gears outside its periphery for reasons of its actual use as a gear in measuring astronomical events. With a little imagination, we may envision the entire circle of the labyrinth lifting up out the ground as a giant cog, being brought up to the heavens like the city of Enoch to join the celestial gears that turn through the eternities. Interestingly, across the Atlantic in the Museo de Arqueologia y Etnologia, in the Mayan Classic Period collection (250 A.D. – 900 A.D.), there is a disk motif of three concentric circles with what seems to be cogs on the outside. A 5-pointed star is circumscribed in a circle within a 6-pointed star. The 6-pointed star has the same geometry as the Star of David. The 6-pointed star is circumscribed by a circle that is surrounded by ten tau symbols. The ten tau symbols are circumscribed by the largest circle. On the outside of the largest circle are what appear to be 10 teeth of a gear. A truly astonishing find since the number 6 and 10 are the basis of the Babylonian sexagesimal cuneiform based counting system. The disk is not named and is labeled in the museum only as a carved piece of shell.[2]

There are a number of approaches to describing the many archetypes embedded in the Chartres labyrinth. It may be simply expressed in its bare bones form as geometric symbols, more elaborately told in a story or it can be experienced in mystery ritual such as practiced anciently in Eleusis. A story that is big enough to live within may be referred to as myth. By correct

---

[2] Daniel Johnson, Jared Cooper & Derek Gasser, "An LDS Guide to Mesoamerica", 2008, Cedar Fort Inc., p. 33.

definition of the word, myth can be real as well. Indeed the Grimme Fairy Tale of Iron John could be correlated to the symbolism of the labyrinth and cathedral symbols, though discontinuities of symbols always arise and must be accommodated. A mythological story that is not real, or at least is very enhanced by metaphor is the story of Theseus and the Minotaur. There are many different versions but here are the basics.

King Minos of Crete desires to take the throne of his father who recently had passed away. The people however wanted a sign that he should be king. Minos strikes a deal with Poseidon to send forth a bull from the oceans to signify that he is to be the next king. King Minos of Crete promises Poseidon that he would sacrifice the bull-man to the sea in return for having brought him forth. But breaking the agreement, Minos decides to keep the bull in his herds and sacrifice another in his stead. As punishment Poseidon makes the bull man wild and fierce, but also make the King's wife, Pasiphae, fall in love with the Minotaur. Pasiphae, through odd circumstances you can read about elsewhere, bears the child of the Minotaur. King Minos of Crete charges a great architect, Daedalus, with the challenging task of designing and building a labyrinth on the Isle of Crete. The purpose of the labyrinth is to conceal the Minotaur to protect the king's wife from disgrace. After a conquest over Athens in revenge for the death of the King's son, King Minos is given a sacrifice of 7 sons and 7 daughters of Athens every 9 years to feed the Minotaur concealed in the Daedalus' labyrinth. Upon the arrival of the 7 sons and 7 daughters, the King's daughter, Ariadne falls in love with one of the sons, Theseus. Ariadne consults with Daedalus and asks how she might save him. Daedalus counsels that Theseus will need to slay the

Minotaur. Ariadne gives to Theseus a ball of curious thread, woven of gold, that helps guide him through the labyrinth. The curious gold ball is called a *klew*. Theseus, upon entering the labyrinth, ties the gold thread to the door of the entrance. In some stories he has his sword, Aegis, with him. In any case, he finds his way to the center of the labyrinth, defeats the Minotaur. (I picture him wearing a phrygian cap.) He then follows the gold thread back to the exit and successfully leaves the mythical labyrinth and marries Ariadne.

Much could be extracted from this and cross-referenced. But at this point, I'd like to reference Fulcanelli's analysis of the Chartres Labyrinth as found in his work, "Le Mystere des Cathedrales". The labyrinth is referred to as *Le Lieue*, which means the league or generally a unit of measure. Previously there used to be a statue of Theseus in battle with the Minotaur in the center of the Chartres Cathedral labyrinth. In concurrence with Fulcanelli, it is not the connections of Christianity to ancient pagan themes that is of import. Rather, it is the universal truths and archetypes extracted and their helpful application in understanding our own spiritual pilgrimage in the Great Plan of The Lord. Fulcanelli's analysis of Ariadne, however, leads to some interesting considerations. The name, Ariadne, is a derivative of *airagne*, in close proximity to the Spanish araña for spider or the Basque *arana* for "the plum". The Greek verb form means "to take", "to draw" or "to attract" and is equivalent to the properties of lodestone, which is an iron based magnetic ore. In Provencal dialect of southern France, iron is called *aran* or *iran*. Fulcanelli asserts that this is equivalent to the Masonic Hiram, the architect of the Temple of Solomon.[3] The straight and

---

[3] Fulcanelli, "Le Mystere des Cathedrales", 1922.

narrow path to the center of the labyrinth, as represented by the radial line, could be considered to be the "iron rod", symbolizing the word of God. The Liahona, being a ball of curious workmanship and the iron rod play similar yet distinct rolls in Lehi's journey out of the kingdom of Jerusalem where the temple is soon to be destroyed. The iron rod leads the rising star through mists of darkness to the Tree of Life where Lehi partakes of the white fruit that is the Love of God. Again, as we look to the stained glass window beyond the third arch, we see the depiction of Adam and Eve in two accounts. In one of the depictions, the fruit of the tree is white.

While we are considering the surroundings of the Chartres Cathedral labyrinth area, let's consider the two pillars to the North and South of the labyrinth. While these two pillars aren't particularly different than any other pair of pillars in the cathedral in their manner of architecture, they generally convey an important message about the sustained duality that exists. Contemplation of the symbolism of "the two pillars" is valuable in understanding much of the thinking around gothic cathedrals and temples in general. Entrance to Solomon's Temple is met by two pillars, as well as by water and fire. The two pillars are as the two horns of the Minotaur in some regards. In some art depicting Theseus in battle with the Minotaur, there are two people standing at the entrance to the labyrinth one on either side of the gate. Often pillars represent people and at times people represent pillars. We can take a look now at the story of Icarus as it relates to the two pillars theme. And a little further on we will compare this with a story that you will hear while taking a tour of Roslyn chapel in the small town of Roslyn outside of Edinburgh in Scotland.

According to Ovid in Metamorphoses, Daedalus was locked away in a tower by the King Minos to keep him from revealing how it is that he built that labyrinth. However, Daedalus desired very much that his son be free of the Isle of Crete and so he crafts for his son a pair of wings with string and wax so that he may fly off of the island to freedom. Daedalus counsels his son to avoid going too close to the sun lest the wax melt and his wings fall apart and he also counsels to avoid going too close to the water to avoid all of the perils associated with landing in a sea while wearing a wax and feather based flying apparatus. Icarus, being young and full of energy flies up and off of the island but being youthful and ambitious continues to ascend too close to the sun until the wax melts, the wings fail and he falls to his death in the ocean. Here the fire of the sun represents one pillar and the water of the ocean represents another. Balance is found in the middle as prescribed by the wisdom of his father. As found in an arch supported by two pillars, the keystone above balances the weight that rests upon the two pillars. When the sun of the sky and the rain drop are brought together in the sky, the result is the resplendence of the rainbow. The arch in stone may for some purposes and in some mythos take on the same meaning as the rainbow. The keystone in the arch is symbolically equivalent to the iron rod or Word of God. If Icarus had obeyed his father's commandment, he might have maintained a steady cruising altitude. In the April 2007 General Conference of the Church of Jesus Christ of Latter-day Saints, Dieter Uchtdorf relates an important message that could appropriately be applied to the fate of Icarus. He says, "When the captain of a long-range jet passes the point of safe return, and the headwinds are too strong or the cruising altitudes too low, he might be forced to divert to an airport other than his planned destination. This is not so in our journey through life back to our heavenly home. Wherever you find yourselves on this journey through life, whatever trials you may face, there is always a point of safe return; there is always hope. You are the captain of your life, and God has prepared a plan to bring you safely back to Him, to your divine destination. The gift of the atonement of Jesus Christ provides us at all times and at all places with the blessings of repentance and forgiveness. Because of this gift, the opportunity to make a safe return from the disastrous course of sin is available to all of us."[4]

In another story of Daedalus, he is charged to take on a student, Perdix. While walking on the beach with Daedalus, Perdix picks up a fish bone and from its framework gets the idea to make an iron saw. He then has further inspiration to take two iron rods and bolt them together to make a compass. Daedalus becomes furious at the competitive ingenuity of the young man and later causes Perdix to fall off of a building. During his plummet towards the ground, Athena turns him into a partridge and he flies away.

If one takes a 45 minute bus ride out of Edinburgh to the small quaint Scottish village of Roslyn, you can visit the chapel that was built there in the 15th century. Roslyn chapel is riddled with symbolism in its architecture. Like Chartres Cathedral, there is reference to the Virgin at the East end of the chapel which is known as the Lady Chapel beyond two beautifully carved pillars known as the Master Pillar and the Apprentice Pillar. The Master Pillar is the Northern of the two and the Apprentice Pillar is the Southern of the two. The Master Pillar is also known in Solomonic tradition as Jachin or Tsedeq and the

---

[4] Uchtdorf, Dieter F., Ensign, "Point of Safe Return", May 2007.

Apprentice Pillar is known as Boaz or Mishpat. As the story goes, there were two Scottish stone masons that built the two pillars that divide the Lady Chapel from the rest of the chapel. The master mason had built the first pillar and decided to leave to go to Italy to study the designs, skills and techniques of the most contemporary masons in the craft. He left his apprentice to go on his journey to Italy. Unsure if the master would return, the apprentice decided to build the second pillar. (The second pillar is on the left side as one stands in the Lady Chapel and faces towards the Nave. This is the apprentice pillar. It represents the lesser light of the moon. It also may represent the caul of the moon or the arc traced by the compass. Recall that Perdix builds the compass.) When the master finally did return he saw the amazing beauty and skill with which his apprentice had sculpted the pillar, became envious of the apprentice and in his anger killed the apprentice.

When they tell the story on the tour of the chapel, they mention the story may be real or more likely an allegory. The story is indeed interesting in that it accentuates the conflict between the traits represented by the two pillars themselves. Each pillar truly is in opposition to the other, but they work together to achieve a higher purpose. To observe the pillars upon approaching them is to see things one way, likely this may be considered the exoteric. To stand under the arch and look outward is quite a different view. That which was alpha becomes omega and that which is right becomes left and that which was left is now right. This might be considered the esoteric. But how does one cross the divide? This is a primary message that may be taken from the account of Lehi when he sends his sons down to the house of the corrupt and fallen Laban to retrieve from him the plates of gold. The plates contained both the word of God and a genealogy, or record of the dead. It is upon the third attempt to negotiate obtaining the plates that the four sons succeed. Just as Mithras slays the bull, Nephi also slays Laban by sword. Later in the dream of Lehi, Nephi ascends by way of the iron rod to the Tree of Life. The message of victory over trial is a central theme of the journey through the labyrinth as well as the objective lesson endowed upon the head of the faithful in his or her journey through life.

VIII. Candlelit labyrinth at Chartres. Photograph courtesy of Jeff Saward.

A Walk through the Labyrinth: A Meditation

"The way to exaltation is not a freeway featuring unlimited vision,
unrestricted speeds, and untested skills. Rather, it is known by many
forks and turnings, sharp curves, and controlled speeds. Our driving
ability is being put to the test. Are we ready? We're driving. We
haven't passed this way before. Fortunately, the Master Highway
Builder, even our Heavenly Father, has provided a road map
showing the route to follow. He has placed markers along the way to
guide us to our destination." [1]

–Thomas S. Monson

We stand at the entrance to the labyrinth, the arena of our
testing. There is life at the center represented by 6 circles
inscribed by a larger seventh circle. Going back in time we can
imagine ancient Minoans chiseling spirals in hillside stones. We
may imagine the mists of Avalon settling on green hills in the
Southern land of the Angles, obscuring view of the stone circles
where earth and heaven hinge. We too for a moment are as stone
in slow thought and luminous feeling drawn into the circle of
Sheshonq in ancient Egypt. The story of the Minotaur in the
labyrinth comes to life as we imagine Theseus prepared to enter
the labyrinth. The way is open to enter. To the right of the
entrance is a basin of clear water and to the left a torch alit with

---

[1] *Monson, Thomas S., New Era, November 1983.*

flame. Washing our hands off in the water and mesmerized by the flame, we notice an ox at our side. That's foolish, why is there an ox there? Never mind. Forget the ox. Looking down we realize that while turning back from looking at the ox we have just taken the first step into the labyrinth. Another look up to the south cathedral wall we find a straight line of sight reveals the stained glass window depicting Adam and Eve in the moment of their fall and descent. Adam's face draws long with grief. Having crossed the threshold into the labyrinth, we notice a few grains of wheat on the floor and a small hardly noticeable gold thread of curious weave. The walls of the labyrinth are dark, though auspiciously covered in green moss and vines of grapes. From high above there seems to be shadows casting imagery on the walls of the labyrinth, silhouettes of tourists pointing and mocking. As we walk the winding path, it as though night is falling in the cathedral. The coldness makes even the brave shrink, but looking forward there is a bit more grain on the floor illuminated by a small glimpse of light from above. Down the wall at the turn, there lies another small piece of gold thread. In the dark of the mithraim, we hear the screaming and clamor. As through the chaotic panic in the streets of Eleusis we wander; so it is that many have been called on this path before. Looking above the cathedral canopy appears as the rough stone of a cavern, yet embedded in the stone ceiling above are gems twinkling with light depicting a bull, a fish, a scorpion and other beasts. So, we walk the path of the Chartres labyrinth on the floor, contemplating these images. Holding a piece of gold thread in hand, it morphs to become an iron rod. The wall to the left becomes hot with flame. We smite the rock wall of the labyrinth on the right with the rod of iron and water pours out, as flame surges from the left. The flame and water interlace in the atmosphere to become mist; the mist rises and settles in a stillness obscuring the way before us. It thickens around us. Stopping to contemplate this, we recall the father, Daedalus, and the words of wisdom he gave. Holding to the rod, we can now walk a straight course to the center. The sounds of rushing waters issuing from the center and flowing toward the periphery are heard. The mists thicken and become as 7 scorpions lined up to prevent passage to the center. Standing before us in the mist is the second of the 7 scorpions. It stands before us with pinchers extended. Contemplating the pinchers deeply, we consider the two horns of the Minotaur; one as fire, one as water. The Minotaur is before us. Dichotomy? The Minotaur stands wild and fierce. With his exhale, steam issues from his nostrils. However, hmmm…we are thinking. We sit down on the floor to have a good think about all of this. After all it's a meditation. While sitting and contemplating the dual nature of the human experience, the Minotaur gets bored and says, "Hi, my name is John." That's interesting. He's not all that scary really. "John, eh? Where are you from?" The Minotaur responds, "Yorkshire". "Isn't that where they make the puddings?" we respond. Snorting puffs of mist in the cold labyrinth, John the Minotaur asks, "What's your name?" "My name is Aegis bearer, thread finder, riddle solver!" Sounding familiar?

At this point, letting the imagery go, and standing in the peaceful arena of the Chartres Cathedral it's good to consider that false dichotomy is one of the most prevalent fallacies of reason. Living in extremes is one way we encounter the Minotaur. In reasoning and debate (two of the schools of the Trivium), being confronted by a false dichotomy often causes us to react by attacking back or polarizing to one side or the other. Or we may inadvertently accept the false dichotomy as the only two options available. What Lucifer brings to Adam and Eve in the garden is a false dichotomy, albeit the oppositional forces he presents are real. It's true that life requires light and dark, hot and cold, health and sickness, flat and bumpy, feast and famine etc. Nonetheless, these are the outer boundaries only or the two horns of the bull. Holding the compass of Perdix up to the light, we see the horns of the bull at the points. They define the bounds, the periphery, the outermost circle. The solar light of day is one immoveable pillar and the lunar light of night is the other immoveable pillar, as well as the physical and spiritual, male and female. The letter "A" itself is an upside down bulls head. I tend to imagine that the horns of the slain bull may be used as the fixed radius of a circle. Chartres Cathedral's windows each have a large compass design over each window that looks like a fancy letter A. Turning back to the imagery of opposites represented in cathedral architecture as we discussed earlier, we find in the arch that rests upon the two pillars that there is typically a keystone that represents the Word of God. Between the two extremes is everything else in between. The Book of Mormon often uses the grammatical device known as a *merism* and will present two opposites, but the spirit of the message is to consider all that is in between the two extremes. In Chartres Cathedral the Word of God is represented in the pillar architecture by the intersection of two circles. This forms the geometric representation of the *vesica piscis,* which means fish bladder. Likened to the counsel of Daedalus to his son to avoid the extremes of fire (sun) and water (ocean), the symbols that are equivalent such as the thread of Ariadne or the iron rod in Lehi's dream, are symbols of the Light of Truth or the Light of Christ. The message here is that our own reasoning is always limited and finite. Our reasoning alone without the Light of Christ leaves us in the dark and we never are born free of the labyrinth. But through Faith in Christ we may transcend the abyss that we encounter in our finite journey through our time on Earth. By the *Grace* of God and His *Mercy* are we saved.

Regarding John the Minotaur, that part of the riddle is solved, he clocked out, defeated by reason, and went back to his home in Yorkshire for a tea, probably with a little honey and a side of locust pudding. We may now enter the center of the innermost circle. There is a genuine reverence for the work and sacrifice done by others that has helped us understand this much, the little that we really do understand. The steady work and toil that our forefathers and mothers put forth bears fruit unto the 3rd and 4th generations. Their love for their posterity is an unseen warm blanket that falls upon us. We feel a blossoming in our hearts, the "desert blossoms as the rose" within us, warmth in our hearts, as it were, the warmth of the noon day Sun. Taking a moment we give thanks to the Lord Jesus Christ who descended below all things and ascended above all things, that we may overcome our trials and tests. Where we have failed, He has made up the difference, where we are lost he holds out a hand to guide us through. But what of 1260? It was the inquiry of this journey? Perhaps the answer is, in part, found in Ether 12:6, which reads: "And now, I, Moroni would speak somewhat concerning these things which are hoped for and not seen; wherefore dispute not because ye see not, for ye receive no witness until after the trial of your faith."

As we turn to make the journey back to what is now the exit of the labyrinth, we lift up our eyes and look upon the fields, always striving to have the image of the Savior in our countenance; for the fields are white already to harvest[2], as white as a harvest moon. And as we do look upon the fields in their resplendent whiteness, we, in fact, look up towards *the west* portal of the cathedral and behold there is the rose window in all of its beauty. All of the intricate stained glass parts ornately orchestrated and working together to sing the song of wholeness to the eye, iconographically imaging the pilgrims' path with Christ at its center within the central circle within circles of the great rose window, Christ is depicted as the judge. Unlike the other rounds in the window gearing, Christ is depicted in a round that is partitioned in 4 parts, yielding within the central circle a central square. "For God doth not walk in crooked paths, neither doth he turn to the right hand nor to the left, neither doth he vary from that which he hath said, therefore his paths are straight, and his course is one eternal round."[3] After a restful walk back through the labyrinth in solemn contemplation, we pass the four corners of the labyrinth circle. Weaving through the quadrants of time and the crucible of affliction, even the gestation grounds of a pilgrim's progression and the testing ground of the gods, we consider that faith, hope, charity and love, with an eye single to the glory of God qualify him for the work.[4] The expressions of the *love of wisdom* of honest and humble men and women in the roots of our ancestry, as limited as they may seem to be in our judgment, need not be discarded as chaff under the great light of the new day, but rather acknowledged as what in all probability was more than an acceptable offering in the judgment of God in their time. If we

---

[2] D&C 4:4

[3] D&C 3:2

[4] D&C 4:5-6

in our day stand tall, it is because we stand upon the shoulders of the great; their images carved in cathedral stone; small, hunched and having neither form nor comeliness that we would desire. They each bear the weight of their cross, hard work and sacrifice; and their bones are in the crypts below foot, beneath the cathedral, some having spilt their marrow into the soil of labor's toil that would bear fields of white, under great duress.

We look up to the left to the window of Eve, the help meet for Adam's need; for whom Adam gave a rib indeed. We are humbled that the Good Shepherd leads us each through. But what of the red fruit and white fruit of the Adam and Eve window? "Come now, let us reason together, saith the Lord: though your sins be as scarlet, they shall be as white as snow; though they be as crimson, they shall be as wool."[5] "Remember faith, virtue, knowledge, temperance, patience, brotherly kindness, godliness, charity, humility and diligence."[6] Walking the slow spirals in a relaxed meter, we near the exit, next to the metaphoric grains of wheat on the ground of this contemplation, we notice a grape lying on the ground, no grape falls to the ground uncounted by the Lord. We are back at the threshold about to exit. The knee bows, the tongue confesses his name. We stand up to take the last step to exit past the two sides of the labyrinth gate. Upon entry all that was left is now right and all that was right is now *left*; and, thusly, we *leave*. As the right foot comes forward with the right hand in front of the stride, we look up and see the Tree of Jesse Window in colors of red, white and green with 7 depictions ascending towards heaven, leaves restored to the tree in its fullness. As our heart feels full of joy for

---

[5] Isaiah 1:19

[6] D&C 4:6

having walked the Jerusalem mile, we feel at the back of our left heel a pinch as the labyrinth gate closes and seals. We leave it in the Lord's hands. Whatever that pinch at the heel was probably was not any of our business (or you could say it was none of our bee's wax). We keep our eyes fixed on the Tree of Life and stand tall. As the sun is setting in the West side of the Cathedral, the beams of light pass also through the emboldening stained glass depiction of Jesse's posterity rising upwards towards heaven, led by the Savior.

But what was that pinch at the heel? Ok. Let's take a time-out to consider this. There was also at the instant we exited, a grumbling in the Earth. As we were passing the threshold of the labyrinth circle over circumference and gear teeth, the outer perimeter of the great stone circle grumbled closed and the gear spacing became complete and uniformly equidistant. The left and right labyrinth walls, metaphorically fire and water, closed together, fire and water combining to form steam; the power source that turns the wheel of the locomotive. As the circumference necessarily decreased in its corresponding measure, the arc angle from the origin to the opening decreased. The inner circle was sealed off and the 6 circles are finally in perfect symmetry! As the arc angle from the center to the periphery decreased in circumference it appeared for an instant, as it were, to be the trump of an angel, expelling the air under the pressure formed by the fusion of the two opposing walls (fire and water) within. As that *arc angle* or *arch angel* is in the process of leaving the circle, the air is blown through the trump and the sound goes forth to fill the immensity of space. The spiritual journey in and out of the labyrinth itself maybe compared to air being inhaled by the labyrinth and exhaled upon departure. The labyrinth itself in this context is as a lung and the aperture or gate from whence the hero departs is, as it were, the mouth of the Lord or the mouth of the Lion. Sealed by the Tau and offered to the Lord, the 6 circles in the center now form two triangles. They are interlaced as the marriage of spirit and matter is now organized and in balance as symbolized by the Star of David. I like to believe that eventually the whole labyrinth in its four quarters is eventually lifted up into heaven as was the city of Enoch, to join the great gears and cogs that the bodies celestial roll upon in awesome wonder. (We might even imagine the number 6 itself rolling up like a scroll tight like a 0 and tied off with a red bow like a Christmas wreath.)

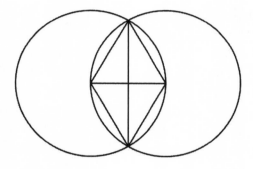

IX. Vesica Piscis

The geometric symbol for three is the triangle. The triangle is begotten of compass and straight edge on paper from the two circles and line segment. The line segment represents the seed of male divinity and the two circles represent the female divinity. The triangle with point down is the alchemical symbol for water because water flows down to Earth from whence it originates. The triangle with point up is the symbol for fire; this is because, like the candle flame, fire goes up to the heavens from whence fire originates. The two triangles are another geometric manifestation of the "opposition in all things" taught by Lehi.

The first and second arches, together, bring to mind the realm of "things which act"; of fire and air or the spiritual world. The third and fourth arches, together, bring to mind the realm of "things which are acted upon"; the things of water and earth or the physical world.

So that concludes contemplation of Arch 3 matters. I once had a boss that would ask me for the status of my work projects by asking, "Is everything lined up and squared away?" Excellent question as we move to Arch 4.

The Fourth Arch

"And it came to pass that the thirty and fourth year passed away, and also the thirty and fifth. And behold the disciples of Jesus had formed a church of Christ in all the lands round about. And as many as did come unto them, and did truly repent of their sins, were baptized in the name of Jesus."

-Nephi 4 Nephi 1:1

As we did the thought experiment of walking the labyrinth, like a thief in the night, unbeknownst to ourselves, we passed into the domain of the fourth arch. All that is East of the center Rose in the labyrinth is under the fourth arch. As we discussed before, there is an incommensurable irrationality about the labyrinth that is reconciled in a successful contemplation while walking it. A mathematical treatise would rely on pi. We found deep in the mythos of the labyrinth the evidences of the value of the *triangle*, the geometric representation of 3, meaning *three angels*. One important triangle in this experimental meditation was in the form of a geometer's compass, as devised of iron by the apprentice of Daedalus. We found another interesting geometric artifact manifested as the thread of Ariadne, the iron rod, which symbolizes the Word of God and the attractive force of lodestone. The iron rod helps guide the pilgrim safely through. The iron rod may be considered the Chief Cornerstone that descends from Heaven and may be represented as a line segment. The iron rod is begotten into finite time and space, or the *temporal* plane (physical plane), from the two legs of the compass. As such, the base of the triangle becomes the cornerstone of the geometric square. The humidity of a warm day may find itself divided during the darkness and cold of night into air and the watery dews. The morning sun rises to find the purified dews distilled upon the leaves of the tree; so too the doctrines of the priesthood distill from the heavens above upon those who have garnished their thoughts with virtue.[1]

In 1260 A.D. the Chartres Cathedral was consecrated and named, "The Cathedral Church of the Assumption of Our Lady". This cathedral, consistent with the movement in France at the time, emphasizes feminine deity. Circles are associated with the feminine attributes. Both the English word *church* and *circle* are derivatives that flow from the same Old English root, *circe*. This is equivalent to the Germanic *kirch* and Latin *circus*; the same root of *circumscribe*.[2] In the New Testament, the bridegroom will return to the bride. The bride symbolizes the church. So with this emphasis on femininity in the labyrinth as a whole symbol, the masculine symbols in the labyrinth are, with reason, the minor presence and are expressly the lack of the feminine. This enigmatic way of expressing the unifying relationship between otherwise oppositional masculine and feminine symbols pivots on the fact that the Latin word for milk is '*lac*'. It is the Latin letter "T" which was originally drawn as the Greek cross, "+" that manifests masculinity in the labyrinth. Reading between the lines is what we might typically say; in this case we are reading between the curves and we are finding between the curves the "+" sign. According to Harold Bayley, the

---

[1] D&C 121:45

[2] Harper, Douglas, *Online Etymology Dictionary*, www.etymonline.com

Celtic words for father were *tad* or *tat* and are equivalent to the Egyptian *tat*, *dad* or *daddu*. The *tat* or *djed* is an Egyptian representation of the four pillars.[3] Phallic in nature, like the stem of Jesse, it represents the backbone of Osiris. Interestingly it is the apprentice of Daedalus (dad) that designs an iron saw fashioned after the jagged backbone of a fish they found while walking on the beach. The four horizontal disks in the boughs of the Egyptian djed represent Osiris after his 14 parts were scattered across the land. Well, ok, more particularly they represent 13 parts of Osiris; his wife kept one. In the Joseph Smith papyri found in Abraham Facsimile 1, there are four canopic jars depicted under the altar. These again represent the four pillars. The Egyptian djed is a symbol of a tree, much like the Ashera stone. The Ashera was a phallic stone that is a commonly found ancient motif. Though generally phallic in shape, the Ashera is a depiction of the mother goddess of the Canaanites. The Tree of Life envisioned by Lehi is at one level a representation of the virgin mother and the child Christ.[4] Nephi's enquiry to an angel about the tree of life symbol is answered with a vision of the virgin mother in white, as the bark of the stem of Jesse is also depicted as white. The yin and yang relationship of masculine and feminine collaboration seems to be present in each of these stories and the symbols that depict them.

[3] Bayley, Harold, "Lost Language of Symbolism', 2006, Dover Inc., Vol 1., p. 353,354.

[4] Peterson, Daniel C. "Nephi and His Ashera", Journal of Book of Mormon Studies, 9/2(2000), p. 16-25.

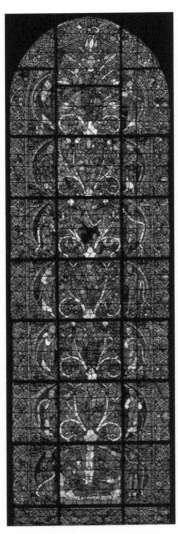

X. The Jesse Window

Since we are looking at roots in general, be they geometric, genealogical or etymological, we now look back up to the Jesse Window on the right hand side of the Rose Window. Unlike the rose windows that contain stories in circles, such as the round window associated with the third arch that depicts Adam and Eve just after having eaten the fruit, with Adam clutching his throat; to the contrary the Tree of Jesse lineage is depicted in squares. There are seven of them.

The Jesse Window shows Jesse, the father of David, in the first and bottommost square dressed in a red robe. He is reclining on a couch with an amazingly prosperous posterity springing upwards towards the heavens from his loins; each of six descendants being lifted up in the boughs of the tree is depicted in their own square. While each seems to stand on top of the tree, each also becomes the trunk of the tree like a pillar supporting the next. Branches wisp out from below their perch downturned in spirals; much in the fashion of the Fleur d'Lys (flower of fire or light). Squares 2 through 5 are 4 kings of Jesse's posterity; each wearing a green robe over the right shoulder. In the 6th square is Mary, the mother of Jesus; and the Lord Jesus Christ is in the 7th and most ascended square, he has a red robe over the left shoulder, a green robe over the right shoulder and is coronated around the head.

XI. The Tree of Jesse window at the West portal, Chartres Cathedral.

"And there shall come forth a rod out of the stem of Jesse and a branch shall grow out of his roots." (Isaiah 11:1)

What is transmitted from above in light, filtered through stained glass windows, is imaged below in stone. There are four inferred radii in the labyrinth that suggest the straightness and rectitude associated with the rule of four kings of Jesse's posterity; three have green robes over the right shoulder signifying government resting upon the shoulder and one of which is a temple builder; that being Solomon. Notice that the girdle tied around the waste of Solomon is gold and appears as an Egyptian Tau symbol. There also appears to be three sapphires adorning Solomon's robe as referenced in the Song of Solomon found in the Old Testament. There is also a sapphire in his golden girdle. In the Invocation of Isis to Osiris found in the Burden of Isis, Isis invokes the god of Osiris as the god of turquoise and Lapis Lazuli.[5] Notably the skin of Osiris is described as being as iron.

The stem referred to by Isaiah, is more specifically the trunk of the tree. The rod that comes forth out of the stem is the rule

XII. King Solomon in the Tree of Jesse Window.

of the four kings as represented below in the labyrinth as four radii extending in the four cardinal directions: east, south, west and north. The stem is thusly the seventh and center circle that the 6 smaller circles are enwombed within. The Latin word *virga*, means *staff*, but also may mean stem, branch or trunk. The trunk of this tree is white. "Behold the virgin thou seest is the

---

[5] Bayley, Harold, "Lost Language of Symbolism", 2002, Dover Publications Inc., Vol 1, pg 213.

mother of the Son of God..." says an angel to Nephi. Nephi then says, "And it came to pass that I beheld that she was carried away in the Spirit; and after she had been carried away in the Spirit for the *space of a time* the angel spake unto my saying: Look! And I looked and beheld the virgin again, bearing a child in her arms."[6] I'd reckon from these symbols that the *space of a time* has a relation to the symbolic meanings associated with the numeral 6. The time that Thesius was in the labyrinth was also likely a measure that is related to 6. In the Tree of Jesse window, Mary is the 6th square and her son, Jesus, is in the 7th square yet depicted in 6 segments; 3 above his solar plexus and 3 below.

Jesus is the child of Mary. Depicting the body of Christ in 6 parts seems to show a parent to child relationship. The child is a part of the parent. Furthermore, with 6 circles in the labyrinth found within the seventh central circle and considering the wording of Nephi's vision of the virgin having been carried away for the space of a time, space and time as represented by planets and planetary motion comes to mind. As such, each of the people in the ascending tree may represent heavenly bodies. In Pythagorean number symbolism four is considered feminine and creation in the temporal and physical plane. Thusly numbers within squares seem to indicate the temporal seat of spiritual bodies. Keep that thought in mind; we'll refer back to this at the end of the book. But as planetary bodies, one may typically assume that in classical astronomy and symbolism, Jesus represents the Sun or vice versa the Sun represents Jesus. There seems to be an alpha and omega relationship with Jesse and Jesus here. The virgin is the 5th of Jesse's posterity, which confirms the numeric relationship of the number 5 to the virgin as well as the

---

[6] 1 Nephi 11

planetary corollary Venus. Venus traces a 5 pointed star with respect to the Earth over an 8 year period.

There are seven white doves surrounding Jesus encircled in gold rings that are connected to the tree by white branches. However below the knee of Jesus seems to be three additional symbols making 10 in total. This appears to carry the same archetypal meaning as the 10 Sephiroth in the hermetic Qabalah.

XIII. Nine circular rings branch from the body of Christ with the 10th in the place of his footstool, the earth.

The base of the tree and its buddingly circular sinew geometrically appears as a reflection of the essence of the geometric positions of the top three white doves and each appears circular. The 10th would be the circular footstool that is the stem; the Earth upon which Christ rests his feet. Each of these 10 circles may be considered a "sphere of creation" and an emanation of light from the presence of God. Moses writes the words of the Lord regarding his creation of the Garden of Eden, "And out of the ground made I the Lord God to grow every tree, naturally, that is pleasant to the sight of man; and man could behold it. And it became also a *living soul.*" For it was spiritual in the day that I created it; for it remaineth in the sphere in which I, God, created it..." Each sphere of creation is unique in its attributes. Pythagoras taught that "there is humming in the strings, there is music in the spacing of the spheres." He taught that the planets all emit a "hum"; this is referred to as *musica universalis*. 2500 years later, NASA has confirmed that the planets do emit vast ranges of vibrations as Pythagoras postulated. Though the waves and hummings are not naturally audible, waves such as plasma and radio waves may be converted into sounds and are publicly available to listen to courtesy of NASA. The humming of Jupiter was recorded in January 2001 by the spacecraft Cassini.[7]

After having deeply considered this emblematic artwork many times and having moved on thinking I'd extracted all that could be, in a later consideration it suddenly seemed inescapable that the tree itself looks much like bone and sinew. At first I thought that was just a strange perception of my own morbid conjuring. However, upon another good pondering, it seemed to makes some sense. The tree grows upward through posterity from the loins of Jesse to the crown of Jesus. While this clearly depicts the tree as the phallus of Jesse or a source of procreation of posterity, it also appears to represent or suggest a correlation with the spine. The pedestals that each of Jesse's posterity stands

---

[7] www.solarsystem.nasa.gov

upon appear to be as if they were bone or even as if they were vertebrae, with the ancestor below standing as a pillar. The human spinal column is symbolic of the World Tree or Axis Mundi. In Egyptian iconography, the djed seems to have equivalent meaning as the Jesse tree window. The Egyptian djed is as a pillar or tree with four levels representing the spinal column of Osiris. In tantric tradition, energy rises up from the base of the spinal column through chakras to the crown and is symbolized by a serpent referred to as Kundalini. The spinal column symbolizes strength, hard work and moral fiber. It also represents the ladder that ascends to heaven and back down again.[8] In this case Jesse is in the Kundalini location or root chakra and Christ is in the Crown chakra location. As there are seven people depicted in the Tree of Jesse along what appears to be a spinal column, so too are there seven chakras in the Eastern tradition. Kundalini is symbolized as a coil or spiral, because a coiled serpent would have the "potential" to move to spring. Reflected below in stone, it would be reasonable to see the coiling turns of the labyrinth to be representative of that coiled serpent. As it was the case that Moses placed a serpent on his staff and held it up as a contemplative device for those in need of healing, so too the savior Jesus Christ was lifted up on the cross, that he might provide healing and atonement. In the Greek world, the staff or rod of Asclepius is depicted as having a snake wrapped around it. Asclepius was the Greek god of healing. The staff as a symbol is equivalent to Caduceus and often represents Hermes or the Roman god Mercury. The caduceus is entwined with two serpents, seemingly in opposition of each other. When Jesus was crucified, he was nailed to the cross with a thief on

---

[8] Nozedar, Adele, "The Element Encyclopedia of Secret Signs and Symbols", p. 575-576.

either side of him. A thief is one who robs justice. They are as two serpents with Christ in the center as it were the keystone or third pillar between the two pillars. In this sense Christ is symbolic of the spinal column and of healing. In the Pearl of Great Price, the Abraham Facsimile 2, figure 2, shows a bull headed man with two opposed faces with a staff in his left hand. In addition to the vertical staff itself, there are three supporting legs making a total of four supports upon which a four legged animal stands. A derivative of the two horned and two faced bull-headed man is the baphomet head, legendarily attributed to Knight Templar initiation and ritual. Similar to the caduceus, the baphomet is depicted in the hermetic art of Eliphas Levi as having a sword with two serpents spiraling helically around it, located such that the sword denotes the phallus. Once again, reflected below in the stone labyrinth is a correlating symbol to the phallus; the labyrinth as the navel or *omphalos* represents the center of the Universe. It is the place where "health" is taken in to nourish the child that is yet to be born. So both male and female body symbols are working together emblematically; both the light through the window and stone jointed by air. In terms of body symbols, the Tree of Jesse is in duality both a phallus and a spine and even Jesse himself is turned away, perhaps at the immodesty of the situation, or more likely in grief his own carnal nature, but the erect phallus and spine seem to denote a 90 angle. Many Egyptian hieroglyphs of royalty depict this bodily geometry. These are symbols of rectitude and righteousness. In the stone labyrinth, the phallus is opposed by the vaginal or *labial* traits of the labyrinth, the birth canal, the womb, the nurturing environment where all of the parts are brought together in water to grow into unity, circumscribed into wholeness. When brought together, these symbols denote resurrection, rebirth, restoration, life, family and fertility.

The Four Elements

We see again that the windows and stone are working together in harmony to tell their story. Before flint and steel were used to start a fire, iron and stone were used. Fire dwells within all things; it is attributed to Hermes by Agrippa and to Dyonisius by Francis Barrett that fire is found in the following particular words: "in all things and through all things."[9] By striking the stone with the iron rod, fire may be extracted. Discovering this principle of arcane value draws attention to our recollection of Moses who struck the side of the mountain and not fire, but rather water issued forth, emblematic of birth or rebirth. But even yet, fire is in the water. These are lovely complementary emblems. The phallus of Jesse illuminated with the fire of light and the feminine symbols of water and womb in the stone labyrinth are unified by air. But how is it that fire is in water? Fire is in water when water is in its form as mist; as the mist that surrounds the tree of life. Here is a critical consideration: to begin to separate the mist into its ancient elements of fire and water is to begin to see the tree, and thusly fire and water as separate elements are as the two pillars that are at the entrance to the path leading to the mysteries of God.

It's important to acknowledge that Francis Barrett's wording describing fire and earth in The Magus is very close to the

---

[9] Barrett, Francis, "Magus", 1801, reprinted by Samuel Weiser Inc., 2000, p. 75.

wording used by Joseph Smith in teaching about the atoning work of The Son of God. Francis Barrett says, "Fire, *in all things and through all things* comes and goes away bright" and Joseph Smith describes Jesus Christ, the Son of God, as "He that ascended up on high, as also he descended below all things, in that he comprehended all things, that he might be *in all and through all things*, the light of truth; which truth shineth. This is the light of Christ. As also he is in the sun, and the light of the sun and the power thereof by which it was made. As also he is in the moon, and is the light of the moon and the power thereof by which it was made. And also the light of the stars, and the power thereof by which they were made and the earth also, and the earth also, and the power thereof, even the earth upon which you stand...which light proceedeth forth from the presence of God to fill the immensity of space".[10] Francis Barrett goes on to describe a 4 level system of elements with fire being in the highest most active position, air being the next active element, with water as a passive element and earth in the lowest order also being passive.

Often the study of the mysteries of God is termed as "the occult". I have always found this word to be unnerving until I found out what it really meant. It means the hidden things or things that are obscured from view. The sun is "occulted" from our view during a solar eclipse; this is a time when the moon moves in front of the sun, blocking our view. The Proto-Indo-European root *kel* means to cover or conceal. *Ob* means "over", like the moon passing over the view of the sun or as found in the word *ob*struct. So 'kel' and 'ob' together mean something like "concealed over". Without vowels, the consonants are KLB. The

---

[10] D&C 88:6-10, D&C 88:12

Latin word "celare" means to hide. *Occulare* derives from "ob celare" and thusly from occulare the word "occult" evolved. Interesting extensions of the root verb celare are found when we consider that the root *kel* or *cel* are their basis. Cel is the same root as in *celo* or *cielo* meaning heavens.[11] The *ceiling* of a great cathedral or temple might represent the coronating realm over the firmament that is associated with the stars above. Celestial would also come from this root. The celestial kingdom could be considered to mean "the hidden kingdom". The word *seal* also comes from celare. For this reason we read the heavens were sealed and so forth. While in jail, Joseph Smith prayed saying, "Lord God Almighty, maker of heaven, earth and seas and all things that in them are...stretch forth thy hand; Let thine eye pierce, let thy pavilion be taken up, let thy hiding place be no more covered..."[12]

The four classical elements of fire, air, water and earth are used to poetically and metaphorically describe spiritual principles. The Lord himself relies on these teaching devices. Our human experience is limited. Our words are limited. With all the technology we have today, why would we still resort to such a simple scheme for describing eternal principles? Well, we can definitely use newly developed phrases like "electromagnetic wave propagation" to describe the same thing that the ancients might have described simply as "fire". But it's likely that more of us can relate to the warmth of a campfire than we can relate to "electromagnetic radiation". So, symbolic use of the basic elements can go a long way.

---

[11] Harper, Douglas, *Online Etymology Dictionary*

[12] D&C 121:4

After Joseph Smith was killed by a mob, Brigham Young was sustained as prophet, seer and revelator by those westbound temple initiates who had begun their spiritual journey to progress to become like the gods. Brigham Young taught, "What is a mystery? We do not know, it is beyond our comprehension. When we talk mystery, we talk about eternal obscurity; for that which is known ceases to be a mystery; and all that is known we may know as we progress in the scale of our intelligence. That which is eternally beyond the comprehension of all our intelligence is mystery." "These are the mysteries of the Kingdom of God upon the earth, to know how to purify and sanctify our affections, the earth upon which we stand, the air we breathe, the water we drink, the houses in which we dwell and the cities we build, that when strangers come into our country they may feel a hallowed influence and acknowledge a power to which they are strangers." "If you say you want mysteries, commandments and revelations, I reply that scarcely a Sabbath passes over your heads, those of you who come here, without your having the revelations of Jesus Christ poured upon you like water poured upon the ground." [13]

---

[13] "Teachings of the Presidents of the Church, Brigham Young", 1997, p. 257-58.

The Square

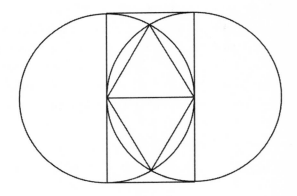

XIV. *The square may be drawn from compass and straight edge.*

Let's return to a geometrical contemplation on the Chartres labyrinth and consider that each of the four radii may each be considered to symbolize a rod. The rod in this case typifies the rectitude of kingly rule, justice and linear measure. The quadrants of the labyrinth circle insinuate the squareness, so we may imagine the four rods extending radially, leaving the radius to the judgment of God. Thusly, the length of the rod multiplied by itself is the area of a square or the area of one of four quadrants. When multiplied times 3.14 or pi, we find the area of the circle. In the window each of the 4 royal members of Jesse's posterity, may be typified by the 90 deg square symbol. Jesse is lying horizontal, and his male lineage extends upwards at a 90 degree angle to his spine. Each of the 4 kingly sons are at 90 degrees to Jesse. Thusly they form the square below that extends outside of the perimeter of the circle. Branches tend to be younger than the trunk. In the Jesse window the branches spiral as in nature branches do. If I could track the path of my children as they run around the house, I have no doubt they make more spiral turns in a day's journey than I do.

While there are various patterns of labyrinths found in sacred places throughout the world, the pattern at Chartres is distinguished by the four implied radii. While only curves exist in the actual stonework, the four radii show that in the progression of man, there is effort to observe order within chaos.

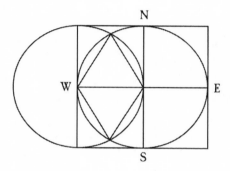

Figure XV. The square represents the Earth in its four quarters. Four cardinal directions are depicted above.

Modern masons may use the term *ordo ab chao* which is Latin for "order from chaos". In the extremes of nature, a spiral may be observed in the tornado and hurricane. In the center of the tornado and hurricane is what is referred to as the eye. It is a peaceful place where forces are balanced; light may be seen in the eye.

Osiris and Abraham: An Omega and an Alpha

A horse is a symbol of kingly ability. It gives the king velocity as expressed in physics by the variable "v", that is should the horse be harnessed under his reign, in a manner agreeable to both horse and rider. The horse stands on four legs in the same manner that the kingdom stands on the four cardinal directions.

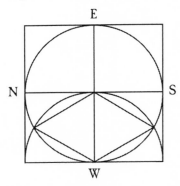

XVII. The two triangles that represent the duality of the Roman Janus, the Egyptian principle of Ma'at, or the two headed eagle can be brought together point–to–point.

XVI. The two triangles observed within the vesica piscis may be brought point–to–point to represent the Druidic axe or labrys. As an axe it symbolizes division. It also symbolizes the mending and unifying nature of the bow.

Each of the 4 insinuated radial line segments of the labyrinth also define where and when the path continues through the quadrant. Where the path is terminated, the dark space on the radius appears to look like a *labrys*. The labrys is a two-sided *axe*. Each of these axes turns the unprepared pilgrim back. Each axe symbolizes the angels that stand as sentinels to guard the *way* to the tree of life. We don't typically picture sentinel angels wielding axes. This is more of a Gaelic or Druidic symbol. It is equivalent in function to the sharp sword that divides asunder both soul and spirit, joints and marrow and discerns the intents of the heart. Imagery arises of Anubis weighing the heart of the dead against the feather of Ma'at, the goddess of truth, justice and order, upon entering the Hall of Two Truths. At this

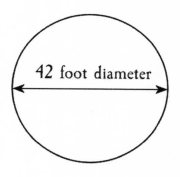

XVIII. 3x14 ft. = 42 ft. diameter of the labyrinth symbolizes the 42 questions of purity of the full measure of universal law.

point the deceased pilgrim is evaluated against the principle of Ma'at or the two truths. Osiris keeps the gates. There are 10 labryses seen in black stone in the labyrinth, as it would be by the 10 commandments that the Sons of Moses would be prepared to meet the face of God, being bearers of His priesthood. Or in the Egyptian ceremony, the candidate would be asked 42 questions regarding their purity and obedience to eternal principles and laws, perhaps even covenants before Osiris, who holds authority and each of the "grand Key words". Each radius represents various levels of obedience and accountability. Here the meaning of the 42 foot diameter of the labyrinth is revealed.

Each of the four rods, or rather each of the four line segments defining the four quadrants of the labyrinth, represents the Word of God, the justice of God, the judgment bar, and it is Osiris that keeps the gate. We can deduce that since Abraham is given the "Grand Key Words" according to Joseph Smith, Osiris and Abraham share a common role. Osiris is spread over the land in 14 parts as are the 14 generations of Abraham until Jesse. 3 x 14 parts of Osiris are represented as the 42 foot diameter and 3 x 14 Generations of Abraham to Jesus of Mary is represented by the 42 foot diameter. It appears that Osiris may actually have been Abraham. The resurrection of Osiris by Isis and the gathering of the tribes of Israel are types of the same principle; that principle at the most divine level is the Atonement and Resurrection of Jesus Christ.

2/3 of the posterity from Abraham to Jesus of Mary is visible to the viewer from Jesse to Jesus as metaphorically depicted above as the Tree of Jesse in 28/42 generations. And 1/3 or 14/42nds are not embodied above and is thusly invisible above, yet that geometry shows up in the geometry of the stone below, suggesting that not only is Osiris-Abraham not embodied above at this time, but considered to still be at work below in the underworld. The Egyptian Duat, is the underworld, the world of the dead or known in Mormon theology as the spirit world of ancestors, which is also the realm of the genealogist; and so too symbolizing this realm, are the 1/3 of the posterity of Abraham, including himself, which are veiled to the observer. Christ descended below all things that he might be in all things and through all things while in the Garden of Gethsemane. After he was crucified on the cross, he descended once again; this time to preach to those who yet have attachment to their misdeeds. This would suggest that not only was Osiris-Abraham engagedin the work of exercising judgment at the axial gates of spiritual progression but also in preparing souls to repent, exercise faith and live obediently to the 42 principles of exaltation. This is a work that Christ was known to have done, known both by his disciple Peter after the time that Christ had been crucified, as well as known in latter days. Peter writes, "By which also he went and preached unto the *spirits in prison*; Which sometime were disobedient, when once the long-suffering of God waited in the days of Noah, while the ark was a preparing, wherein few, that is, eight souls were saved by water." (Peter 3:19) The Mormon prophet Brigham Young taught, "Where is the spirit world? It is right here...Do [spirits of the departed] go beyond the boundaries of the organized earth? No, they do not...Can you see it with your natural eyes? No. Can you see spirits in this room? No. Suppose the Lord should touch your eyes that you might see, could you then see the spirits? Yes, as plainly as you now see bodies."[14] Thusly according to Brigham Young it would be true that spirits remain within the boundaries of the organized earth. Joseph Smith discussed the ancestors in the realm of Abraham-Osiris, "The spirits of the just...are not far from us, and know and understand our thoughts, feelings, and emotions, and are often pained therewith."[15] The understanding of the underworld is not occulted in the teachings restored through the seer Joseph Smith, rather directly and openly taught and in a manner so clear that the true spirit of the matter may be felt, even the Spirit of Elijah. It seems that Joseph Smith may have

---

[14] Widtsoe, John A., "Discourses of Brigham Young", p. 577

[15] "Teachings of the Prophet Joseph Smith", P. 361.

considered that Abraham was one and the same as Osiris, as it appears to be clear to the great architects of the Chartres Cathedral, and possibly clear to some few dedicated families that imparted of their substance in order to build Chartres Cathedral. Though complexly occulted in a labyrinth of symbols during the 13th century, this principle of the spirit world is by no means occulted to modern Mormons. It is taught so clearly that a small child could tell the story. Until recently it was held that 1/3 of the threefold mission of the church is to *redeem the dead*. To do this, Mormons search deep into their ancestral roots to find the *names* of those that have passed on and perform sacred ceremonies in their behalf; but only inside the temple. Regarding the work done in the temple for both the living and the work in behalf of the deceased ancestors, Brigham Young taught: "Your endowment is, to receive all those ordinances in the house of the Lord, which are necessary for you, after you have departed this life, to enable you to walk back to the presence of the Father, passing the angels who stand as sentinels, being enabled to give them the key words, the signs and tokens, pertaining to the holy Priesthood, and gain your eternal exaltation in spite of earth and hell".[16]

So, where might the unseen 1/3 of the Jesse Tree be found in the stonework of the cathedral? Where is the unseen 1/3 above in stained glass reflected below "unseen" in stone? The answer is astounding. Below the labyrinth, under the cathedral is a crypt. According to Jean Markale, the crypt is older than the cathedral itself. It contains wells that were dug deep into the earth deep amidst the roots of the ancients, from whence waters may be drawn; the waters that flow from the roots and the roots

---

[16] Young, Brigham, *Journal of Discourses*, Vol II, p. 31.

of the ancient ancestors. The wells were built by Druids. Markale's research demonstrates that the Celts believed in a spirit world beyond the veil. It was symbolized as being under the earthen mound called a *sidh*.[17] The spirit world was known as the "otherworld". It is a transitory place and place of waiting, though it is timeless. It is described as paradisiacal. On the day of Samhain, the veil between the objective earthly plane and the spirit world of the sidh is thin, and interaction with the dead is considered to be a more simple transaction. It is in the Celtic Samhain celebration where bobbing for apples in a barrel of water on October 31st originates. The apples exist partly above in air, and partly below in water; specifically the fruit of the tree resides at the veil between water and air.

The labyrinth as a whole is a symbol of birth, a journey through womb waters, and Carl Jung viewed the labyrinth as a symbol of the unconscious; those things we are not aware of...yet. By entering and journeying through it, whether in the microcosm or in the macrocosm, we gain more consciousness or in other words further light and knowledge.

To end things up on the ground floor, we see in the labyrinth the 3 insinuations of straight lines, the axes of sentinels, the demands of justice. The 4th straight line, the one that opens to the West, by which none pass, is the Word of God Himself. The number of labryses in each line could be considered symbolic of the family of Christ. Of the 4 radii, the North and South contain 3 labryses, the East contains 4 and the West effectively has 5. 3 represents Osiris, 4 represents Isis and 5 represents Horus. Horus typifies Christ. Three, four and five

---

[17] Markale, Jean, "Cathedral of the Black Madonna; The Druids and the Mysteries of Chartres".

make a Pythagorean triangle, which contains the "right angle" or a 90-degree angle. These relationships also show up in Egyptian hieroglyphs.

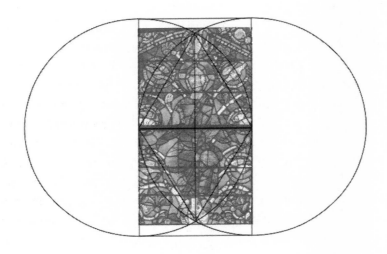

XIX. Geometry shows that Jesus is depicted within the bounds of 10 smaller circles (sephiroth) that define the atoning section of the vesica piscis in the Tree of Jesse window. Photo by Dr. Stuart Whatling PhD and geometric graphics by author.

The Four Legs (The Throne of God)

The square represents a generally masculine attribute in geometry; it represents man's journey and walk through life. The square also represents man and woman's earthly experience, which includes everything that could possibly happen here as we progress faithfully in the footsteps of The Way. The square particularly represents the godly walk; the walk that Jesus walked and that Adam desires to walk. However, life itself tends to rest in the comfortable and uncomfortable chair of 4 legs. Whereas Isis is represented in the Pythagorean 3-4-5 triangle as the leg of the triangle that is 4 units, our spirits sit in the seat of the material world. Its four legs are the classical elements themselves; Fire, Water, Earth and Air. When we use the term "elements" we typically modernly think of the periodic table of about 118 elements. However, anciently the 4 basic elements that constitute the seat or throne of life were much more expansive in meaning. Fire could be considered to be literally fire, but also anything like unto it such as the *spirit of God* or the Word of God, it could represent the sun that warms the day or the refiner's fire that separates the dross from the silver. It may represent lightning, laser light or a gift. Water may represent anything from two parts hydrogen one part oxygen, to a cup of water, to anything that acts like water, such as a solvent that causes dissolution, the Waters of Nun, the waters of creation that were moved upon, water is a common symbol of dreaming and night time as the mind experiences a dissolution in order to assimilate information, which then takes form and is tried against the fervent noon day heat of the day. Water is the birth place of much creativity. Water is the atmosphere of our primal home in the womb of our mother. Earth and Air too have their meanings ranging from the most literal to the most poetic and spiritual. When we talk about these elements, we can relate to them, they invoke emotions. When we use Cesium 137 radioactive decay as a poetic device, it just doesn't get my wife's attention as much as saying that time is beating with the fervent passion of a heart on fire. Yet both are elements of life on earth that count out time. The chemical elements rest on the periodic table and the periodic table yet stands on four legs.

These four legs are the throne of Isis that are the matter (latin *mater*) into which our spirits are born. Three squared plus four squared gives birth to five squared. These squarings all represent the spiritual or infinite being coupled with the *temporal*, meaning time limited or finite. Thusly, the spiritual is being woven lovingly into a *matrix* of *linum*. In his treatise on the Grimme fairy tale, Iron John, Robert Bly asserts that it is from under the pillow of the Queen or *mother* of the kingdom that we find the key to freeing Iron John, or rather below the pillow yet above upon *mattress*. These matrices and mattresses are the bed of life and Bly's poetic vision invites us to a profound contemplation on where to look for divine guidance. When Jesus met a man who lacked power or strength, who could not believe that he himself without the help of another man could walk to the moving water as swiftly as the others, Jesus said unto him; "Rise, take up thy bed and walk". And when the man heard this from Jesus, he found strength to take up his bedding, mattress and all, and walk. This was not a lesson on self-reliance but rather on reliance on the Word of the Lord. Jesus was a manly man, but more importantly a fatherly man. He did not carry the man to the water source, however, his word to the man was as living water. He truly understood how the man's fears kept him from going to the water. To the contrary, Jesus's cousin, John, was a wild man; a man that took other men and immersed them in the water. In another epic moment, Peter took up his metaphoric mattress and attempted to walk with Jesus, however, the water alone in that hour of the fourth watch did not sustain him in entirety. Jesus was, in fact, sustained by water as he walked on the stormy sea to extend his hand to Peter, and it was the waters in which Peter began to sink. This demonstrated to Peter that Jesus was called to be the next leader of the church after John the Baptist had died. It also demonstrates that the power of the priesthood depends on the sustaining power of the feminine which is manifest as the body of the church. He, Jesus the Christ, did have the keys of the priesthood and He who atoned for man did sustain Peter and extend his hand to Peter to which Peter could hold and walk uprightly.

Interestingly, in the Celtic myth of King Arthur, Arthur breaks his sword due to misuse. After repentance, after all that Arthur could do, it was the Lady of the Lake that could restore to him his sword. It was water that returned to Elijah his axe with no handle.

Conversely, when Lot's wife looked back to Sodom and Gomorrah, she turned to a pillar of salt. Salt itself is waterless. She had nothing with which to sustain her husband.

It might be said, that when a man can take up his mattress, and accept responsibility for the life that he has been given and accept his maleness, then the power that is weak in the fourth leg, is given strength by the Lord Himself. And unto what end? To be a father, a husband and a servant of God and good; to protect and feed His sheep. The fourth leg is a shared leg. And the measure of its strength will be a reflection of the strength that we give unto others.

The Return of the Woman

After our meditation upon the labyrinth, we can envision it as being a closed circle, sealed tight like a *crucible* with the Star of

David defined in its center core by the geometry of the 6 circles. The influence of the iron rod or Word of God over the four corners of the earth is reflected by radii that extend to a length that creates a square interlaced with the circle with area equal to the area of the circle. The equivalence of the area of the circle to the area of the square implies balance. To accomplish this with no more than the use of a square and compass is the classic Greek geometric problem called "Squaring the Circle". To do so mathematically, the measure of the rod or line segment needs to be slightly less than the radius of the labyrinth so that metaphorically the balance between male and female, bond and free, old and young and all above and below are living according to the demands of justice, with the required measure of mercy, after all man can do. And holding all the pieces of a kingdom, people, land or a person, such as Adam, together where there is any fracture or any wound and filling every jot and tittle of the law that the abyss may be transcended, is the atoning blood of Jesus Christ. And by his *love* and his *grace*, we are quickened.

The fourth pillars complete the third arch and begin the fourth arch. The pillars are stone and the space in between is air, thusly at the beginning of the fourth arch is the establishment of the spiritually created in the physical plane. The fourth pillars on either side of the labyrinth bisect the core in twain. The plane of the labyrinth and the pillar constitute a 90-degree angle. The 90-degree angle is measured by the carpenter's square, as Jesus was a carpenter. Jesus would have also worked with stone, which would mean he was also a mason. It was in the fourth watch of the night that the authority of Jesus Christ was confirmed to Peter and the apostles, after John the Baptist had been beheaded under the Herod *tetrarchy,* whose judgments came from his corrupt wife, through his daughter, rather than by enlightenment of

God. This dichotomy strongly emphasizes that Jesus had authority from God, as demonstrated by reaching forth his hand to Peter as Peter began to sink in the fourth watch, Peter himself having not been sustained by the water.

While each of four squares are as the four pillars of the Egyptian Djed, the four sons of Lehi, the four kingly rulers in the stem of Jesse, the four cardinal directions of the zodiac, the four cornerstones of the temple; they are also as the four cornerstones of the restoration of the gospel in the latter days and thusly represent the Priesthood after the Order of Melchizedek. Interestingly, the Congregationalists of early American history, led by men such as the British exile separatist John Lathrop of Barnstable, Massachusetts, organized congregations where people would meet, and where each could talk about their spiritual beliefs in Christ. These Congregationalists acknowledged that no man had any authority greater than another man. Their view was that there was no authority from God on earth at the time. Some anticipated a restoration.

The latter-day thinker may wonder while reflecting upon the Chartres labyrinth if there was an awareness as power moved from the homelands of Gaul to the broad thin wings of Roman rule, that the four pillars were not to be found in their fullness, but were with hope, yet in the seed of Jesse. Perhaps there were some in the times of 1260 A.D. Chartres, France that were aware that they lived in the wilderness of times, in anticipation of the dawning of a new era and the restoration of all things, including the priesthood dispensed with authority from God. Since the consecration of the Cathedral occurred in that year, I would suspect that they were hopeful for the rise of the morning star and the return of the Son of God to Earth.

"And she brought forth a man *child*, who was to rule all nations with a rod of iron: and her child was caught up unto God, and to his throne." (Rev 12:5)

"And the woman fled into the wilderness, where she hath a place prepared of God that they should feed her there a thousand two hundred and threescore *years*." (JST Rev 12:6)

And so we are brought to consider the 1260 year cycle.

"And he shall rule them with a rod of iron; as the vessels of a potter shall they be broken to shivers: even as I received of my Father. And I will give him the *morning star*. He that hath an ear let him hear what the Spirit saith unto the churches" (Rev 2:27-29)

And thus the discussion of Arch 4, the true tetrarchy in the seed of Jesse and the square concludes. *Valete!*

Supper's Ready

OK, there it is, there is the relationship we were looking for on this journey to Chartres Cathedral. 3x14=42 is an expression that is a puzzle piece inside of a much larger embodiment of cosmic modeling. Joseph Smith Jr. of the early 1800's America saw it and so have several others. Now you have too. Certainly all the pieces are not resolved into a crystal clear image of how the cosmos works, but look at how many things we've encountered on the way! Lest any further mystery ensue, let me make it clear that my journey to Chartres Cathedral was in fact real and not an allegory. Furthermore, unlike figures like Christian Rosenkreutz, my friend Greg Miller is not in any possible way allegorical; he is a real fly fisherman who knows how to gracefully get around Europe.

As the evening began to fall upon us, Greg and I left Chartres Cathedral. We stopped by a quaint gift shop and picked up a few post cards and souvenirs. We then went to look for a good place to have dinner. For whatever reason I don't recall seeing a single French restaurant. Those crepes back in Paris might have been good at this point. We found a small kebab restaurant and had supper. I have found that the kebabs all over Europe are by far my favorite travel food. They typically come with French fries, can be purchased for less than 10 Euro or English pounds or whatever and are delivered quickly enough to eat, feel satisfied, then get on to the next adventure.

After supper, Greg and I then took the train back to Paris. I would imagine I took a nap on the ride back. I don't recall. I was pretty tired.

Perhaps where this story leaves us in France in 1260 A.D., we can imagine the events that are soon to transpire. In a small bookshop in France in the 1300's, a simple man receives a curious book with strange hieroglyphs. The book cannot be read but must be translated. The name of the book is "The Book of Abraham, The Jew" and the good man that it comes to is Nicholas Flamel.

The Crossing at Chartres

The stone and stained glass messages and imagery of Chartres Cathedral express more than a well-articulated voice from the dust. There is a timeless harmony; the song of geometry. A family of standing waves is orchestrated into the stonework like the humming notes of a choral masterpiece. And where there is a note, there also is ratio. It's hard to imagine how important that mathematical ratio was in art, science, philosophy, architecture, deistic ritual and in the schools of cathedral design. The cathedral makes evident the manifestations of the powerful secret geometric codes that the traveling stone mason guilds of the Middle Ages kept within their sacred craft. The stone buttresses atop of the cathedral extend like an ascending clockwork of stone gears and cogs into the heavens, engaging with the cycles that carry the stars and planets in their seasons; the celestial bodies all moving in proportion the one to the other. The harmonic cycles of Venus and Mars attested then, as they do now, that there truly are amazing proportions in the life-sustaining design of our solar system. When the Great Architect laid compass and rule down to draft the times and seasons of mankind, great care was taken so that His fallen children might also find joy. The symbols in Chartres cathedral emblematically conspire together to tell stories and teach veiled truths about the cosmos and man's fallen yet divine roll in the Great Plan. While there are many stained glass windows and stone depictions well worth consideration, let's take a look at how just two of them may be brought together upon the altar of thought to make visible the familial relationship of all things.

The Tree of Jesse window and the labyrinth can be married together to reveal some delightfully fruitful contemplations upon the divine plan of the Great Architect.

Let's first re-examine a few of the attributes and meanings found in the labyrinth as a symbol. Firstly it is a symbol of gestation or motherly nurturance. Conversely it is a symbol of the trials, challenges and perils of growth and birth. It is a symbol of Earth itself; whole yet divided into its four rudimentary parts, whether elemental or seasonal. As a circle it models the mathematics of cycles. Its association with gestation invites all properties related to fertility and monthly cycles; the lunar calendar and moon rule over all the symbols subject to her. The earth rotates obediently on her axis, revolves around the sun and provides all that is needed to sustain life to her children. To poise our thinking for what's coming up in this contemplation, let's consider the lost 10 tribes of Israel as being the fruits of the great tree and children of Mother Earth. Though the 10 tribes are broken apart and scattered, the labyrinth symbol emphasizes the maternal care under which they are garnered and gathered as a hen gathereth her chicks. Our thinking and imagery must move with agility from the poetic to the numeric symbols of both the rational and irrational as we consider that the labyrinth symbol circumscribes into one great whole all truth, including the mathematics of Euclid, Pythagoras, the Greeks, Egyptians, the Hebrews and the Persians. In the case of Hebrew and even English mathematics, etymological linguistics is inseparably woven as gematria into the deeper meanings. In the center of the labyrinth, or Mother Earth, is the inner circle and when sealed closed the geometry of the inner circle may represent the Tree of Life. It also therefore represents "the Love of God". This inner circle may be associated with the presence of the dove on the one hand and the raven perhaps on the other. The raven of Noah flies from its center arc out and over the watery depths, as does the dove. Imagine the circumference of the inner circle of the labyrinth to represent being in the presence of the tree; this is the stem. The tree has roots: etymological roots, historical roots, divine roots, genealogical roots, geometrical roots and so on. It is as ancient as time itself. The linearity of a rod or lineage extends radially from the center, core or stem of the labyrinth to any radial distance from the central origin. We might imagine that fruit falls from the far reach of the boughs under the draw of gravity to the roots at the circumference of the circle that the labyrinth defines. To picture this we do need to imagine the labyrinth sort of growing out of the plane of the stone flooring and into a living tree in the midst of the cathedral. Once again, clear the buzzing tourists out of the Cathedral Nave; look out…we're thinking again. And so the stone floor breaks up as a tree grows up in the very center of the labyrinth. The bark is white and its trunk grows straight up along an axis extending upward from the floor as if the Great Architect just placed a straight edge in three- dimensional space, drew an axis straight up from the center of the labyrinth. Immediately following, two spiraling serpents spiral upward along the axis like the helical DNA of life until the narrow trunk of a tree takes form. The tree's roots surface through the stone flooring growing outward towards the perimeter of the inner circle of the labyrinth. The small tender branches grow outward as the tree grows thicker in the stump and higher as it climbs upward toward the night sky with the highest branches pointing upward toward the seven stars of the Pleiades. The branches grow extending radially in the air above seeming to reflect the burly twisting roots permeating the stone below. The walls of the labyrinth are still mapped in the planar space of the stone flooring amidst the permeating burly twisting roots. The tourists move aside frantically knowing not from what they run and they seem to have their view of the tree obscured by gentle mists that veil their view. On any other day that might be the case for us as well, but today for this discussion, the mists are thin and the view is not obscured. To keep our metaphors clear, the stem is the trunk of the tree. The spirits of the ancient fathers and mothers are in the roots and under soil. The roots run deep into the depths of the earth to drink water from its wells. The branches are covered with green leaves, shimmering as they take in air and catch the sun and moonlight from the skies above. From under the roots issue forth, towards the four cardinal directions, four streams of water that flow down from the central circle to flow to the four corners of the earth. The seeds of love are the attractive force of the Word of the Father, they are placed in the hearts of the children, that when fallen are moved to the far reaches of the labyrinth circumference. They never leave the circle. They are in the mother's arms. The attractive forces of laws, such as the 10 commandments, are represented by the iron rod that grows out of the stem and extends as the loving hand of the savior to the fallen children of mankind at the furthermost circumference of the labyrinth circle. The radius is the iron rod, and it has smitten the stone labyrinth in four locations. The fluence of the four streams of water defines the four quadrants of the labyrinth which may also be considered to be as the four facets of the great Egyptian pyramids. As such, the four streams of water may also be considered to reflect four streams of light above, descending from heaven down into the Cathedral Tree of Life. Sir Isaac Newton writes that a Tree may represent a Kingdom, a Man, a Beast, a Planet and so on. Going along with that sense of the symbol, the labyrinth could be a family tree, or a family of adopted members or an ark or maybe a beehive.

Let's now consider some of the attributes and symbols of the tree of Jesse window. After a concerted contemplation on the spiraling circles of the labyrinth, the straight edges and squares denoting masculine attributes are immediately evident. Jesse's large stem is competitively male. As a contradistinction, the geometric representation as four radii at 90-degree angles in the labyrinth is actually entirely devoid of any straight edges, only those that are implied in the spaces in between the squiggles. Otherwise the labyrinth is entirely curvy. It clearly predominantly represents feminine attributes. To further contemplate the interaction between the Jesse Window and the labyrinth we can consider the two emblems to be likened unto the *two pillars*. The labyrinth would be associated with the Apprentice Pillar and the Tree of Jesse window would be typical of the Master Pillar; or as the Boaz and Jachin pillars of Solomon's temple. As representations of the basic physical elements of water and fire, the labyrinth is most associated with water. Jesse and his Tree are most associated with fire. The labyrinth bears the waters of birth and nurturance. These are the waters upon which Noah and his group were carried to safety and the earthly waters over which Lehi navigated his boat. In Egyptian thought, Horus navigates his boat across the sky over the waters of Nun. Meanwhile, the rectitude and straightness of the fire pillar associated with the Jesse Tree, may be found symbolized as a pillar of fire on a stone, the lightning bolt of Thor, the Light of Christ, the Word of God, the Spirit of God like a fire that is burning, the flaming sword, Excalibur, Logos or I imagine in Eastern tradition as Kundalini. The word *fire* and *fir*, as in fir tree, have common etymological roots stemming from the Greek *pyros,* which builds upon the same root, *pyr,* found in the word *pyramid.* The root of the word *pineal* and *pine* are common. The fire pillar being expressed as the four cardinal radii, being in and throughout the labyrinth is particularly meaningful in that it is fancied that the Merovingian kings had additional ability to "see" clearly throughout their kingdom over their familial stewardship. This would earn them the Greek name *derkesthai* or "one who sees clearly". It is from derkesthai that the word dragon is then derived. Dragon in this sense is quite good, in the same manner that the serpent on the staff of Moses, or caduceus is a symbol of healing. This type of seership is the sort that Moses received to behold "the earth, yea, even all of it; and there was not a particle of it which he did not behold".[1] The Lord established the bounds of what Moses could "see clearly". The word "comprehend"[2] is used by Joseph Smith to describe the Lord's unity with all things, in which case, omniscience is seemingly more than purely visual for the Lord, there seems to be a more kinesthetic element. The all-seeing eye of the Lord is an ancient symbol both found on the Mormon temple in Salt Lake City, Masonic temples, in Rosicrucian tradition and back through history to the Eye of Horus of Egypt. Noah sent out a raven to dry the land and a dove to discern what was happening in the earth. This sequence could reasonably be considered to be likened unto "seeing" at a distance. Joseph Smith used the Urim and Thummim to aid in his seership. The two stones held in the bows were described by Lucy Mack Smith to be two triangle shaped stones, which I would imagine brought together would form the six pointed star. The six-pointed star

---

[1] Moses 1:27

[2] D&C 88:41

may be considered a symbol of bringing together male and female divinity into balance. The Jesse Tree symbol may be generalized to also represent Father in Heaven while the Labyrinth symbol may be generalized to represent a Mother in Earth. This all leads up to what becomes of all questions in the Book of Mormon, one of great esoteric importance. It is a key to unlocking the mysteries of God and discovering the keystone message of Chartres Cathedral. Nephi desires to see the Tree of Life vision that his father saw and, as a result, he is visited by an angel. The angel then asks this key initiating question in 1 Nephi 11, "Knowest thou the condescension of God?" The bringing together of the Father in Heaven and the Mother on Earth reveal the keystone. The keystone is Jesus Christ.

A Chemical and Celestial Marriage

"Therefore shall a man leave his father and his mother and shall cleave unto his wife and they shall be one flesh"
-Abraham 5:18

Let's keep in mind that in the imaginative contemplation of the Tree of Life growing up in the center of the labyrinth, the four cardinal directions became also four streams of water or also four streams of light; perhaps four streams of water issuing from the roots and four streams of light issuing from the heavens. Let's now affix the symbols of the Jesse Tree to the symbols of the labyrinth. We will call this "crossing" them. The Latin root of the word cross is *crucis*. It is also the root of the word of *crucible* as in a chemist's crucible. It often takes on the meaning of bringing things together or making them at-one. Bringing male and female together in this same sense is to *marry* them, as in marrying the two ends of a rope. It also seems to symbolize that anything attached to the four elements of this Earthly material world will become finite and mortal, as it was the case that the Father of Jesus was eternal and the mother of Jesus was finite and mortal. In modern chemistry, stoichiometry is the ratio of the parts of chemical compounds that make up the compound and it is ratio that we will find here at an accelerating pace as we discuss these light matters that coagulate out of this crucible of thought.

The "cross" in the Chartres labyrinth is only represented as dark-space or rather "void" between the winding paths of the labyrinth. It is very much in the similitude of the representation found in the geometric depiction in John Dee's Theorem XVII in The Hieroglyphic Monad[3]. In Dee's geometric theorem, he notes that the each of the 90-degree right angles may be viewed as an L, which is the Roman numeral 50. Or if you tilt your head 45 degrees to the side, you can see the same symbol as a V, which is the Roman numeral for 5. The numbers 5 and 50 are unified by

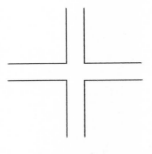

XX. *John Dee's Theorem XVII*

a multiplying factor of 10. The + sign may be viewed as an X which is 10. The four 90 degree angles separated from the point of origin discontinues their unity and they become quaternary, yet the space in between is like an optical *vein* through which light is in *flux*. *Vein* seems to be an etymological play on the

---

[3] Dr. John Dee, "The Hieroglyphic Monad", 1564.

word *vine*, through which the grape is invigorated with nutrition and by which the grapes of the vine are unified in a similar manner to how the veins in the human body unify the members of the body. The LV and X form the Latin word LVX or LUX, which is the Latin word for light. "This is the philosophical light, which you have been informed, was produced by the Great Architect on the first day," writes Dee[4]. The number 10 symbolizes "all of a part".[5] Recalling our world tree is broken and scattered into 10 tribes amongst the 4 corners of the world, bringing them to the cross is to gather them into one or to restore unity. The ratio of ten parts gathered in one among four facets suggests that the flux of light is conjoined at the Tree of Life through four orders of creation and is divided into 10 distinct parts are represented by tribes. This is a beautifully illuminating conjunction of thought. The eye senses light.

Discovering the L, V and X symbols numerically expressed as 50, 5 and their ratio of 10 respectively, we find these symbols are closely associated with the crucis and would be significantly meaningful without any other reference, however, the numeric pair shows up once more in one version of the story of Adam and Eve. In an Egyptian version of the Adam and Eve story translated from Arabic, the First Book of Adam and Eve cites God clarifying to Adam that 5 and 1/2 days to Adam are 5000 and 500 years. God then promises Adam that in 5000 and 500 years, "One" would come to "save him and his posterity".[6] In this case, the L and V or 50 and 5 factors are expressed as multiples

---

[4] Ibid.

[5] Gaskill, Alonzo, "The Lost Language of Symbolism", Deseret Book, p. 132-33.

[6] Platt, Rutherford H., "The Forgotten Books of Eden: The First Book of Adam and Eve: Chapter III", 1928.

of one hundred. The best representation of the 100 factor is 10 squared and as 10 squared reasonably denotes "perfection on earth". This refers to the perfect rectitude with which Jesus Christ would live his life. Another view of the 5000 and 500 years might be to look at 5 and 1/2 times 1000. In the Book of Abraham we may extract from the Egyptian cosmology found in the Facsimile 2, fig. 1 explanation, that Joseph Smith writes, "one day in Kolob is equal to a thousand years according to the measurement of this earth." Ten cubed or 1000 denotes the omniscience, omnipresence and omnipotence of God[7], and is in fact the very same meaning as the LVX symbol. It seems to emphasize the "lights and perfection" of Christ. The Hebrew translation for "lights and perfections" is Urim and Thummim. John the Revelator taught that the Earth would become as a sea of glass. Joseph Smith clarifies that the earth would become as an Urim and Thummim to those who abide a celestial law; thusly the earth may indeed be read like a book.

Again five is the number of fingers on the hand and a symbol of a covenant. The Lord covenanted with Adam and Eve to provide a savior to redeem him and their posterity from the fall. The five pointed stars over the windows of the Salt Lake City Temple represent the patrons participating in the temple ordinances. The five-pointed star may be represented by the V and may be considered to be associated with initiation into the lesser mysteries or apprenticeship. The ten to one ratio again denotes that the fall of Adam initiated a breaking of things into its parts and conversely the atonement of Jesus Christ raised on the crucis or cross makes all whole and one again. The number

---

[7] Cook, M. Garfield, "Cornerstones of the Restoration", 1999 Edition, p. 3.

10 as a symbol of perfection is also a symbol of Jesus Christ who was affixed to the cross. To follow the path of the Savior is to progress through all that 10 symbolizes to become like the Master. This is a good stopping point to solemnly consider the expansive meanings of these symbols. Joseph Smith taught that "the place where God resides is a great Urim and Thummim"; a place of "lights and perfections". Similarly a maxim owing to Pythagoras eloquently professes, "Know thyself and thou shalt know the universe and the gods". What is promised to Adam and Eve and their posterity is the promise of eternal life or life after the manner of the gods and the extended hand of mercy to help us progress towards that end. The walk of progression towards perfection while in this mortal life, however, is an arduous walk and through the mists we must pass to follow in the footsteps of the savior. Yet, the Lord says, "If your eye be single to my glory your whole bodies shall be filled with light, and there shall be no darkness in you; and that body which is filled with light comprehendeth all things."[8]

Recalling Lehi's progression through his meditation, he advanced through a wilderness of darkness and waste to stand in the presence of the tree and looked back with a desire that his family would join him. The Tree of Life in Lehi's vision represents "the love of God". If we apply Hebrew rules to the English word Love, it may appropriately be rendered as LV. LV as a square and compass sign when associated with a tree denote the universally natural balance of feminine and masculine principles and all of their children principles. It also may represent the questions we will be asked before entering into the

---

[8] D&C 88:67

presence of the Lord at the last day or we may simply ask ourselves if we reflect the love of God? We find this consistent balance in the patriarchy and matriarchy of Adam and Eve as well as in the Chartres Cathedral symbols of the Tree of Jesse and the Labyrinth.

The Chartres Cross

With the balance and divinity of the masculine and feminine in mind we consider how the two symbols work together. What would happen if we read the two symbols simultaneously like two different instruments playing music together to make one song. Let's work with numbers in this consideration. A first approach in observing the "crossing" of the masculine and feminine symbols in Chartres architecture may reasonably be to multiply the number 7 associated with the masculine squares of the stem of Jesse Tree x the number 6 associated with the feminine circles of the core circle in the labyrinth which yields the number 42. Forty-two may then represent the children offspring which then, as Adam and Eve, fall as fruit from the presence of God to the outer circumference of the labyrinth. 42 ft is the diameter of the labyrinth. That yields 3 x 14 generations of fertility and fruitful posterity. It's a tricky mental procedure, but let's keep in mind that the 6 (matriarchal deity) and 7 (patriarchal deity) when brought together in unity bear the offspring of unity, which may be represented by the numeral 10. The children are as the Ten Lost Tribes of Israel, broken apart from the unity of the family tree. Also remember that the 10 commandments were a simplification of a higher number of laws that came from God. The number 42 and 10 both represent the children laws of the Great two parent laws of God as taught by Jesus; "Love God and Love thy neighbor". This is quite similar to saying this in a funny kind of way to make the point about the number symbols; "Love the 1 and Love the 10". As we saw in the Jesse Tree, there are geometrically circular depictions surrounding Jesus; this again is a depiction of the 10 to 1 ratio. We will see later where the equivalency of the numbers 42 and 10 come into play in Egyptian covenant making and Judeo-Christian covenant making.

We may note that the 6 circles within the core of the labyrinth to the 7 squares in the Tree of Jesse constitute a ratio of 7 to 6. That ratio seems to be accompanied by confirmation since the 6th square up in the Jesse Tree is the Virgin, the 6

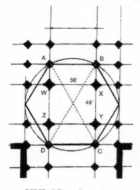

XXI. "Cross" section measurements and image courtesy of John James.

circles in the labyrinth are in the stem or Latin virga. What is amazing to discover is that the 7 to 6 ratio in the "crossing" of the Jesse window masculine symbol with the labyrinth feminine symbol is a ratio that is clearly and firmly established in the geometric location of the pillars of the cathedral! Where the four lengths of the cathedral come together at the "cross" section or in other words where the Nave, the North Transept, the South Transept and the Choir meet there are four piers or pillars. The ratio of the breadth to the length is 58ft to 48ft or in other words a 7 to 6 ratio.[9] Thusly the "cross section" is a geometric ratio of 7 to 6.[10]

---

[9] Strachnan, Gordon, "Chartres Sacred Geometry, Sacred Space", Floris Books, 2003,

These four piers then become the four points around which geometry can then be applied to observe many amazing geometric characteristics of the cathedral.

The cross is a symbol of the atonement of Jesus the Christ. In the Tree of Jesse Window, Jesus is depicted in the 7th square from Jesse, counting inclusively, and the Virgin Mary in the 6th square. In the labyrinth the 6 circles are inside of the one seventh circle. While this center circle is the core of the labyrinth and represents the place of the virgin, in this case, the reference of the center circle may represent the 'rest' of Mary Magdalene. Furthermore, Mary Magdalene may be considered a virgin, made pure through the atoning blood of the savior. At the time of the crucifixion of Jesus, the soldiers took his garments and made four parts.[11] When Jesus was affixed to the cross with his hands and feet nailed and fixed to three of the four extensions of the cross, his mother was there. He hung with a thief on a cross to either side of him. Three men were crucified. Each was as a pillar, with Jesus being the Middle Pillar. Below the cross on the ground looked up to him his mother, who was there with his mother's sister and also Mary Magdalene. The three men above and three women below seem to emphasize the distinct and at times opposing nature of male and female. These two triads may be represented geometrically by two triangles. One represents the divine masculine and the other represents the divine feminine; one as the symbol of fire or light and the other as the symbol of water or earth.

---

p. 62-63.

[10] James, John, "The Contractors of Chartres", Mandorla Publishing, 1989.

[11] John 19:23-42

We may note that two triangles circumscribed by the circle may be found in the geometric locations of the pillars in the crossing of the nave and transepts with three points of the triangle above with point facing down and three points of the triangle below with point facing up. These two triangles point-to-point represent three points of contact, two of earth and water and one common with the triangle below and two of air and fire with the third in common with the triangle above. As we discussed in the previous sections, the two triangles brought point-to-point may be considered to be a geometric symbol of the Tree of Life. So, this section of the nave is symbolically connected with both the central circle of the labyrinth and with the Tree of Jesse. One may say that they are connected in essence.

One disciple lovingly escorted Jesus' mother away at which point Jesus knew it would quickly end. As soon as he was separated from his earthly mother, he lacked water and was thirsty, but in the presence of the soldiers he received vinegar. When he received not water he said, "It is finished". The soldiers then broke the leg bones of the thieves on either side of Jesus. Yet the bones of the Savior they left as intact as his integrity and the justice with which he lived his life in this world. One of the four soldiers pierced his side with a spear and out poured blood *and* water. In some circles of the early church water was partaken as part of the sacrament rather than wine. Joseph of Arimathaea, through the sustaining permission of Pontius Pilate, was able to receive the body of Jesus and take him to the sepulcher in the stone, where the elements of his body would rest for three days. The sepulcher was a stone cavity, covered by a stone door; a womb within the earth where his body would rest while his spirit descended to visit those who were in spirit prison. With priesthood keys given him, his work to do was spiritual; a work of freedom and a work to endow agency upon the spirits of men and women and establish the path for them to become like their Father and Mother in Heaven. On the third day, the stone door was rolled away and Jesus would take up his elements, having parted from his mother and having passed through the veil, to clasp the hand of Mary Magdalene.

Mary Magdalene, still of the elemental order of the earth and bearing the waters of the womb, meets joyfully to embrace her Lord of the Vineyard, who's "eyes were as a flame of fire, the hair of his head was white like the pure snow; his countenance shone above the brightness of the sun and his voice was as the sound of the rushing of great waters."[12] This moment is a great marriage of the heavens and earth brought together at one.

XXII. Interlaced triangles on window of the assembly hall on Temple Square in Salt Lake City, Utah.

The altar may also be symbolized as a tree. The stained glass window found at the Salt Lake City Temple Square chapel shows the symbol of interlaced triangles. It may be viewed as two great triangles interlaced or as 6 distinct combinations of smaller triangles coupled and surrounding the circle. Just as at the death of Jesus, there were three men each affixed to the cross held in the air and three women below, there are three pairs of masculine and feminine triangles paired in the symbol below

---

[12] D&C 110:3

with points shared in order to complete the geometry, making both male and female, as Lehi taught, "a compound in one".

The Bounds of the Priesthood Are Set

The numbers and ratios here tell the stories; they reveal truths. Speaking in English and in the language of number can be challenging to follow, but like any other language it eventually makes sense. Laws irrevocably decried from before the foundations of the earth and heavens[13] set the bounds of both physical law and spiritual law and are in the very architecture of God's plan.

Reflecting back on the quandary as to why there are 4 of Jesse's posterity highlighted amongst the 2 x 14 = 28 generations between Jesse and Jesus. Furthermore, 28 is resolved in Strachnan's geometric analysis as a radius defined by the geometry of the central cross section of the Chartres cathedral. The four sevens or 4 x 7-aspect suggests that the circle of the labyrinth pertains to Jesse's lineage as governing the earth in its four quarters.

Consider that the diameter of the labyrinth is 42 feet long. This 42-foot number symbolism signifies justice or obedience to the natural laws in their fullness and was recognized as being like the governance of the priest-kings over a kingdom. In a more cosmic sense, the diameter represents the rectitude of law, as in "law irrevocably decreed from before the foundation of the earth and heavens". The number 28 extracted from the cross section geometry is also the number of days in the lunar month, thusly

---

[13] D&C 130:20,21

the circle of the labyrinth also symbolizes the four phases of the lunar cycle. So the bounds of the priesthood that are set in the circle are represented by the + sign, the 42 foot diameter and the phases of the lunar cycle. Hold on to that thought for a moment. The ratio of 28 to 42 is reduced to 2/3. "Two" thirds is an even multiple of thirds. "One" third is an odd multiple of thirds. In this case, the 2/3 ratio seems to pertain to the laws of justice and the 1/3 pertains to the laws of redeeming mercy, as applied to the effectuation of the powers of the priesthood; the *laws* of justice and the *law* of atoning mercy. The priesthood must be effectuated within the bounds that are set. In the Egyptian Book of the Dead (1550 B.C.) there are 42 questions that must be answered before entering the temple sanctuary. These are referred to as the 42 declarations of purity. Each of these declarations pertains to a particular law upon which a corresponding blessing would be predicated. Since the diameter of the circle is 42 ft, each part of the whole gospel law may be considered to be represented by a foot of measure. Imagining the wings of the avian depiction of Ma'at extending across the entire labyrinth diameter would express that the breadth and span of her extended wings defines the reach, straightness of the law and balance. In the Joseph Smith explanation of Abraham Facsimile 2, fig. 4, he explains that the dual winged figure (Sokar) is a numerical expression signifying "expanse" and the number he assigns is 1000. We will talk more about the message found in the numerical symbol of 1000. He also notes that this figure relates to time. Joseph records the words of the Lord to him while he was in liberty jail in 1839, "Therefore, hold on thy way, and the priesthood shall remain with thee; for their bounds are set, they cannot pass." (D&C 122:9) Furthermore, "the rights of the priesthood are inseparably connected with the powers of heaven, and that the powers of heaven cannot be controlled or handled only upon the principles of righteousness." The rights and bounds of the priesthood are set and indeed cannot be controlled or handled by the will of man. The powers of heaven may be conferred upon us when we live according to the laws and bounds that are set. In this sense, the priesthood itself cannot be truly abused since it will stop working immediately when the laws and bounds are disregarded. Like a stubborn ox, we would be left kicking against the prick of the cattle prod.[14]

Referring back to Chartres Cathedral, the North Rose Window shows the Virgin with Child Jesus in her arms. She is depicted within a perfect circle, though it is partitioned in twain by a diameter that passes over her navel area, as it was that the veil was rent in twain at the moment of the death of Jesus the Christ. The matriarchy is associated with the veil. At the time that the spirit of a person approaches the veil, he or she will be

XXIII. Ma'at is symbolized here by the scale, but is also present in the dual faced feminine figure to the left of the scale. The heart of the dead is weighed against a feather of Ma'at. Each feather represents a principle. Thoth, with the head of an ibis, is recording the judgment. From the Book of the Dead of Ani, British Museum, London, England.

asked 42 questions of purity. A different god represents each of these questions. It is one feather placed in the balances against which our heart is weighed and Anubis operates the scales. The feathers on the wings of Ma'at each symbolize law. It stands to reason that our heart must be lighter than the full measure of the law; broken, contrite and humble. In geometric symbolism, the horizontal line segment then represents the same balance as the balance in which our heart is weighed against a feather. Jesus taught, "Blessed are the merciful, for they shall receive mercy."

Interestingly, if we now look at the whole earth and consider that it takes 24 hours on the European clock for the earth to rotate 360 degrees. And apply the 1/3 mercy factor to the 24 hours of the day by multiplying 1/3 times 24 we find 8 hours. The Egyptian clock technologies divided the day into 12 hours, one third of which would be four.

The word 'hours' happens to be an anagram of the name

XXIV. A 24-hour clock with the 12 signs of the zodiac in Chartres Cathedral. Photo by Greg Miller.

'Horus'. The word 'hours' is traceable to the Greek word *hora*, meaning a finite unit of time. There seems to be an archetypal boating relationship between Noah and Horus. 8 souls are saved by the mercy and grace of God on Noah's ark. In the Egyptian Sheshonq hypocephalus (Book of Abraham Fac. 2, fig. 3), Horus is represented as sitting in the *seat* or *throne* of God, navigating the waters across the sky bearing the Grand Key-words as were given to Noah, Adam and others to whom the priesthood was revealed. Meanwhile, above in the West Rose window are 24 Elders of Revelation 5:8, holding golden vials. Notably the height of each of the equilateral triangles in the transept "cross" section geometry provided by Strachnan is 24 feet and so a new relationship is discerned. And so the number 24 emerges as an important number symbol in the Chartres model and European model of the cosmos.

These many correlations reveal a connectivity and circuitry to all things. All things may be circumscribed into one great whole. This great whole constitutes a living body. There is a circulation through all things. There is a vital life force that flows through all and is much similar to blood circulation. The cycles that exist all around us are far too numerous for our minds to assimilate even if we could observe them. So, our preference for learning is to break things down into smaller pieces, like the hours of a day and then put the parts together. Even after we go to sleep at night our minds go to work trying to chunk information together. For this reason, we may wake up in the middle of the night with a great epiphany. Our subconscious seems to better deal with non-linear thinking; synching up the essence of things while we sleep under a moonlit and starry sky. However, in the noonday sun we prefer linear thinking; it is something we can work with. In fact, when we use our modern office calendar we depict the day as a square. The days are given finite measure. It gives us the feeling of the partitioning of things; making the infinite a finite thing so that we can behold it with temporal eyes. However, much in life is truly an endless flow and circulation of things. Whether blood, oxygen, energy or matter, it is never truly static. We run into this reality in physics when we try and measure the velocity of a subatomic particle such as a photon. As soon as we know the energy associated with its velocity we lose information about its location and we can only predict statistically where it may be. Or we could choose to determine its location at the expense of knowing its energy. Nature has veils. Nature's veils protect the vital life force that flows through all things. The veils act as boundary conditions. If I try to hold a butterfly, I cannot do so without interrupting the very essence that makes it beautiful; I risk damaging its wings. I cannot pull a rainbow trout from a stream without risking its health. Perhaps it is for similar reasons that we cannot behold the face of God and live. And so prayer in fact may not be a lesser way to communicate with God, but the very most natural way; until we become like him. Veils divide the finite from the infinite. Veils, acting like gates, turn back the pilgrim that is not ready to progress; most often without the pilgrim ever knowing he was turned back. It has been observed that if a person is left alone in a forest, try as they may to walk out of the forest by walking in a straight line, there is a natural tendency to turn to one side which results in circling back. There is likely an analogy about our spiritual progress in this. In Lehi's vision of the Tree of Life, the sacred tree is guarded not by the sharp sword of cherubic sentinels but rather by nothing more than the subtlety of mist. The linearity of the iron rod provides orientation.

So, all of the circulation of life force that we are discussing can be understood and modeled to a limited degree. The natural presence of boundary conditions or veils must be acknowledged and respected. As we discussed in the first arch, "One", or unity, may be represented by a circle but also as a single point; a unifying origin point. Let's look for how time and space are brought together in unity. So, we looked at the 4 x 7 = 28 significance, the cross sign + and the 42 foot span that seems to also represent the wings of Ma'at and the 42 declarations of purity. Let's start to patch this together. Now, it's sort of easy, because we live a thousand years later. We know where things ended up; we know that model that eventually distilled out of this during the age of enlightenment and the restoration of the fullness. Here is the connectivity of all things. We noticed the 4 weeks x 7 days yields the lunar month. The cross symbol or plus sign in the middle of the labyrinth that I was referring to is also a symbol of the temple or Latin *templum*. *Temp* is the root of temporal which pertains to time. 7 days may also represent the geometric cube. Again we find a 6 and 7 relationship here as well. It's like this: there is the up and down axis associated with the architect's *plum*, there is the North-South cardinal axis and there is the East-West cardinal axis. So the set of these 6 directions as a group is numerically represented by the number 6. The seventh is the central origin point that ties the other 6 together into unity! This 7th representation is the rest of the Lord; it is unity. It is also represented by the Tau symbol, which then duly serves as a symbol of atonement in the sense that it holds all of the parts together in unity.

Three dimensions define the cube and the number 7 holds the dimensions together. Thusly 7 and the cube are symbolically equivalent. Each of the four quadrants of the labyrinth represents a "cornerstone". When a stone mason takes a rough stone and crafts it into a perfect cube, it is then called an "ashlar". The word ashlar has common etymological roots with the ashlar tree. The Greek ash tree is a mythological symbol of the origin of man. The ash as a representation of three dimensions is divided by its three axes. We can see how the axe then divides the tree and in the tree there are axes three! This brings us very close to the symbols of the druidic traditions, in particular the three rays of light that constitute the Druidic *Tribann* symbol which may be found in use as a symbol amongst modern druids. The Tribann as a symbol of evocation and invocation brought together become the labrys or dual-headed axe. Notice the amazing power of poetry that is built into the English language. The ashlar stone is also a symbol of man being perfected. Being a cube with perfect facets and symmetry requires at its center, the power of atonement of Jesus Christ. The Tau is the symbol of the forces of the atonement and the unity within oneself that this power brings. The tau and cross are similar and some use the symbols synonymously. The first cornerstone that is laid is the pattern that establishes the location and orientation of the entire cathedral or temple that is build based on it. The Chief Cornerstone is Jesus Christ.

The Labyrinth and the Tree

So the number 7 can represent these 6 directions or 3 axes and their unification. The geometric cube is a good symbol for these three axes as in the case of the ashlar stone. In Hebrew lettering symbols, these three axes are represented as follows: Aleph, Shin and Mem. Aleph represents the Up-Down axis.

The Up-Down axis is also represented by a common tool of the stonemason; the plum. You may have noticed the word "plum" is nestled into the word templum. Aleph is associated thusly with gravity and the fall. The fruit, the plum, doesn't fall far from the tree. When a plum does fall from a tree, it is because there is one thing between the plum and the earth and nothing restraining it. That one thing is air. So that is one way to remember that the Hebrew letter Aleph is assigned the attribute of air. When Adam is born, the breath of life is breathed into him; that is the kind of air that initiates life. Adam initially plays an 'Aleph' roll in the great plan of God as he and Eve step from the precipice of a stable garden of Eden to a fallen state. Aleph in the Up-and-Down sense also correlates with the Stem of Jesse in that man stands erect, which distinguishes him from the animals. Next on the list is the Hebrew letter Shin. Shin is associated with the North-South axis. North and south are polar opposites. My favorite way to designate some attributes to these is based on a Northern Californian/Mediterranean perspective; that is the North is wintery and the South is summery. Shin is associated with the attribute of fire. Forest fires usually accompany summertime in California. Driving through the southwest is a very dry and hot drive. Finally, the Hebrew letter Mem is associated with the East-West axis and is assigned the attribute of water. I imagine the East being associated with springtime and spring rains falling in the green mountain meadows and bringing about flowers. I imagine the West being associated with the autumn Californian sunset low on the horizon over the waters of the Pacific Ocean; for it was from the sierras to the Pacific that the spring rains flowed. The West represents the fall and autumn seasons. So the six directions up, down, North, South, East and West are held together by the Tau.

In the Hebrew alphabet the three letters, Aleph, Mem and Shin are called the three Mother letters. Each of the 6 three-dimensional directions is assigned one of 6 double letters; again with tau being the unifying origin and 7th letter. Double letters are like the two sides of a double-edged sword or the Druidic labrys; each has equally opposing facets built into it. There are 6 figures in the branches of the tree of Jesse; 7 including himself. The stem or trunk unifies them all. The Druids would carve a tau symbol out of an old oak. The tree and tau symbol have comparable symbolism of atonement or unifying power. In corporeal symbolism, the hand represents a tree. The thumb may be considered to be as the stem or trunk and the four fingers are unified by the thumb. The thumb may be thought of as representing the axis mundi and the four fingers as four rivers. In the case of God's children seeking him and looking up to the heavens, the four fingers would represent four rivers of water. In the case of the Lord, looking down upon his children the four fingers represent four rivers of light; just as the pyramid as four edges that join the facets; the axis mundi unites them in the same way the quincunx unites the four facets of the pyramid.

The 3 mother letters and 7 double letters define the perfect cube. We can imagine 6 planes, each being orthogonal to each of the 6 directions, forming a cube with the 7th letter at the center of the cube. Thusly, 6 symbolizes the theological cube. One other aspect of the cube we can consider is the edges. There are 12 edges. Each of these edges has a Hebrew letter associated with it. These are known as the 12 simple letters. Each one is associated with a sign of the zodiac. This adds up to a total of 22 Hebrew letters: 3 mother letters, 7 double letters and 12 simple letters. They define the perfect cube in its dimensional space, the opposition within its axes and all of the edges and the center that

The author at the Louvre, Paris, France, 2010. The geometric quincunx unites the four facets of the pyramid. Photo by Greg Miller.

unify it and make it at one. The aspect ratio is 1:1:1. The Holy of Holies in the temple of Solomon is a 1:1:1 cube geometry;

specifically 10 cubits in every way. Jesus Christ's power of atonement is found in the center holding it all together, at the edges and in its perfection. He is the light that is in all and through all things and He comprehendeth all things. Now is a good time to refer back to the dual feathered figure in Abaraham Facsimile 2, fig. 4 that Joseph Smith assigns the number 1000 to and compare with the expansive wings of Ma'at or that Raukeeyang represents the expanse of the heavens. The expanse that Joseph is referring to seems to be the same dimensional space expanse defined by the 3 Hebrew Mother-letters, the 3 axes they represent and their 6 directions. The 6 directions of the Hebrew Double-letters, expand out from the origin like the double wings of a female mother bird figure. So when the three dimensions of the Holy of Holies in Solomon's Temple are multiplied we get 10 x 10 x 10 or 1000. This is the expanse of Ma'at made at-one by Horus or Jesus Christ. Horus or Jesus Christ is God as appropriately represented in Abraham Fac. 2, fig. 3. So 1000 is the number of a cube that defines the expanse of all things in all dimensions and aspects that are also defined by the 22 letters of the Hebrew alphabet. The dimensional space of the expanse defined by the breadth of the wings of Ma'at defines a kingdom. "All kingdoms have a law given; And there are many kingdoms; for there is no space in the which there is no kingdom; and there is no kingdom in the which there is no space; either a greater or lesser kingdom. And unto every kingdom is given a law; and unto every law there are certain bounds also and conditions."[15]

The 22 letters of the Hebrew alphabet are further used in a Hebrew model of the cosmos that is also called "The Tree of

---

[15] D&C 88:36-39

Life". The Abraham Facsimile 2 in the Pearl of Great Price also represents all that is represented in the Tree of Life. The 22 letters are paths or light-paths that connect 10 nodes. Each of these 10 nodes is called a "Sephiroth". Each node has an attribute associated with it. The 22 letters + 10 sephiroth = 32. There are 32 degrees of progression in the stonemason Scottish Rite. The number 32 finds a gematric place in Mormon cosmogeny when we consider that the primary and central source of light that emanates forth to lighten all creation as represented in the Abraham or Sheshonq hypocephalus, emanates from Kolob.

Just as we saw that the English word "axes" takes on a dual meaning if we consider the two sides of the double-sided axe, a Hebrew letter has an unseen facet. In the Hebrew language each of the 22 letters is assigned a numeric value that carries number symbolism. Just as English words may be poetically crafted to communicate a deeper sense beyond the words themselves, the Hebrew letters and wording can carry a depth that extends beyond the simplicity of the word itself. Were these Hebrew writing devices used in the bible? Possibly so. Why? Because the Old Testament was written in Hebrew. It is inescapably the case that all associated meanings originally accompanied the specific words chosen to be used in Old Testament writings. Unfortunately, even the cleverest of our forefathers typically didn't have such ample access to so many books, libraries and information as our current era has. And perhaps they were better off in some regards without such inclinations to explore the elaborate depths of ancient Hebrew writing. Nevertheless, some clearly did have access to these cosmological literary concepts. But since we do in our era have this info readily available now, we'll look more into these writing devices in a later chapter.

The Ascent

The windows in the cathedral point to the heavens and the heavens dispense the story below. It is the sunlight that filters through them and splinters into color giving vitality to the cathedral. The North Rose Window central core section shows the virgin mother and child. Virgo is closely related to the virgin, particularly as she carries the grains of wheat. It was at the meeting of the church after John the Baptist had been beheaded that they ate 5 loaves of bread and two fishes. The zodiac symbol for Virgo is like an M with a little fish attached to the side of the M. In this Rose window, there are 12 little circles attached and surrounding the core Mother circle. The depiction accentuates that the twelve revolve around the mother circle like the 12 simple letters in the Hebrew Qabalistic alphabet find their centration in the three mother-letters. Some amazing geometric symbols may be found in the heavens above. Venus traces the 5-pointed star in its 8 year cycle. 5 are the numbers of fingers on each hand of God. The hand is used in making covenants between man and God, through angelic ministers. The hand of God coupled with the hand of man adds to 10 fingers. The West Incarnation Window is between the Jesse and West Rose Window and consists of 10 centrally vertical partitions, the highest of which is somewhat broken in its completion. The pattern anticipates from the ground up that the 10th and highest partition would be full and whole, yet the 10th square partition is incomplete and broken, which would leave it *disjointed*. Like the Christ partition in the Jesse Window, the 10th partition in the Incarnation Window is divided with 3 segments and an incomplete 4th in which is the crown of the Mother of Jesus. A crown is also signified by the fleur-de-lis in the utmost segment of the incomplete 8th segment of the Jesse Window. The top part 10th part in the Incarnation Window and Jesse Window, the part that is an incomplete square but sealed off with two arcs is known as the *joint*. The joint is completed by the meeting of the two arc angles, which symbolizes the healing power of the atonement through the Mercy of the Savior.

A similar geometric pattern and number symbolism is found in a bas-relief on the great porch at the Notre Dames Cathedral in Paris[16]. There are 9 squares defined by the *rungs* of the ladder referred to as the *scala philosophorum*. A 10th ladder rung is not present, but in its place, the primitive substance of creation, veiled as the face of the Virgin Mother. "I was set up from everlasting, from the beginning, or ever the earth was. When there were no depths, I was brought forth; when there were no fountains abounding with water. Before the mountains were settled, before the hills was I brought forth: While as yet he had not made the earth, nor the fields, nor the highest part of the dust of the world. When he prepared the heavens, I was there: when he set a compass upon the face of the depth".[17] Taken as a whole symbol, this bas relief of the Virgin Mother, appears as the Greek letter phi, with the ladder being the vertical line dividing the Great "O". Interestingly, this divided O or circle may also be considered to be found in the North Rose window at Chartres. In the North Rose Window there are 12 circles and 12 squares that surround Virgin and Child. We also compare the geometry of the central circle of the Rose window to the circle of the labyrinth, both sharing the commonality of being divided

---

[16] Fulcanelli, "Le Mystere des Cathedrales".

[17] Proverbs 8:21-27

through the center by a diameter. A careful visual inspection of the 12 squares reveals the quincunx with the center point at the location of the Virgin Mother and Jesus! As above, the 12 circles may symbolize the 12 constellations of the zodiac in the heavens above; they also symbolize power to move. So below, they may symbolize the 12 apostles carrying the gospel to the four quarters of the Earth. "And there appeared in heaven, a woman clothed with the sun, and the moon under her feet, and upon her head a crown of twelve stars: And she, being with child, cried, travailed in birth and pained to be delivered."[18] This is the woman that fled into the wilderness. Again, in the central circle, around which all the rest of the angels are surrounded in numberless concourses, the Savior as a Child sits in his throne. The throne upon which he sits is the lap of his Mother, the Virgin Mary. "And to the woman were given two wings of a great eagle". The two wings conjure imagery of the Egyptian Ma'at and duly so.

In France during the 13th century it was, in fact, anticipated by the faithful and righteous that the doctrines of feminine deity would be restored. Mary became a symbol of the feminine principle and also began to be associated with the Greek goddess Sophia. The name Sophia is Greek for wisdom and the basis for *philosophia*, or the "love of wisdom". The attribute of wisdom traditionally assumes a female gender. "Happy is the man that findeth wisdom, and the man that getteth understanding…she is a *tree of life* to them that lay hold upon her." And it is through this tree of life, or wisdom, that the Lord effectuated creation and hath "founded the earth".[19]

---

[18] The Revelation of John 12:1-2
[19] Proverbs 3:13-18

XXV.   The North Rose Window at Chartres Cathedral. Photo by Dr. Stuart Whatling, PhD.

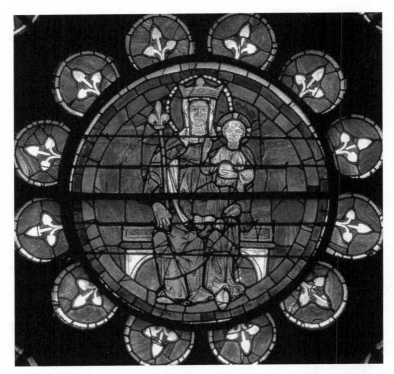

XXVI. The Virgin and Child in the North Rose Window at Chartres Cathedral. Photo by Dr. Stuart Whatling PhD.

The circle is divided in twain at the navel of the Virgin with the Savior in her care. Her right hand wields a staff with the fleur-de-lis in the vertical position while the babe Jesus rests in her left arm. Notably the babe looks much more like a tonsured clergy member than Jesus. Perhaps, this represents "the priesthood" in the arms of *the woman*. Opposite the North Rose Window is the South Rose Window and in the South Rose Window is a similar motif; they are a reflection of each other. In the central circle is Jesus again, seated in a throne that is an actual material chair. This has reference in Egyptian learning as the throne of Isis.

The horizontal line divides him at the navel. His right arm is raised making a hand gesture; his left arm is at his side and holding a golden chalice. In Hebrews *4:12*, we read, "For the word of the Lord is quick, and powerful, and sharper than any two edged sword, piercing even to the dividing asunder of soul

XXVII. In the South Rose Window, Jesus holds a chalice in the upturned palm of his left hand, while his right arm is held vertically.

and spirit, and of the *joints* and marrow, and is a discerner of thoughts and intents of the heart." Thusly, since the gospel carries the attribute of dividing asunder, we wield the number 12 (half of 24) as a divisor into the dividend 42, yielding the quotient 3.5. What works for my thinking is to express it like this: 12 x 3= 36 and 36 doesn't meet the full measure to seal the circumference of the labyrinth geometry, so add +(1/2 x 12) = +6 to yield 42; and the full measure of the law is filled, every jot and every tittle. In the South Rose window, there are three radii of three concentric circles and a fourth that is half a circle, for 3.5 radial regions. The ratio of each circumference is visually intuitive when comparing to the Phaistos disk of Minoa. This is to say that 3.5 is a number that has a more universal meaning that can be identified cross culturally; it may be said that it is the end of the Minoan spiral midway as one walks a straight and undeviating path across the diameter of the spiral. It is interesting that the ancient Minoan disk is laden with mari*gold* flowers. The streets of Jerusalem in John's revelation are described as being paved in gold. So, anyhow, as we were exploring here 3.5 is the sum of 1/2 + 1 + 2 and is referenced by John the Revelator in Revelation 12:6 as "a time and times and the dividing of a time". John is given a rod, which we have discussed as being a symbol of the measure of the diameter of the circle of which in the case of the labyrinth is 42 feet. It is with feet that one walks over the golden streets of Jerusalem. John's vision of two prophets prophesying as they walk the streets of Jerusalem for 42 months establishing the law of God also references the 42 declarations of purity that must be answered before passing beyond the veil according to the Egyptian Book of the Dead. This is expanded by John by a 30 day factor so that 42 months is then expressed as 1260 days. And there it is!

In the "Chymical Wedding of Christian Rosenkreutz", he is invited to attend a wedding. He departs his cottage, which is on the side of a mountain and ascends, passing three gates on the way. After arriving at the kingdom, the candidate is weighed on a scale. This part of the allegory reflects the same type of spiritual judgment as having one's heart weighed on the scales against a feather of Ma'at. Only those candidates that pass the judgment may go on to attend the wedding.

The Birds and the Bees, the Milk and the Honey

In the Doctrine and Covenants we read, "In the celestial glory there are three heavens or degrees." The division of the highest ascensions may be noted in the segmentation of Christ's partitioning in the Jesse Window. There are 3 partitions in rectangular form, the top rung of which passes through Christ's navel area and there are three more defining the areas of the heart, head and in the highest partition is a dove. The dove is 1 of three parts in the same manner that the Holy Ghost is one of three members of the Godhead. In the 12 circles in the North Rose Window are 12 winged beings. 8 of which are regular angels with wings and 4 are doves. Thusly the 4 doves again represent 1/3 of the 12 winged beings. The 8 angels represent 2/3 of the winged beings. Outside in the third circle are 24 angels...the ones with the golden vials. The 2/3 and 1/3 ratio shows up consistently.

"On a table breast high to the Magi were on one side of a book or a series of golden pages or plates and on the other side a vase full of celestial-astral liquid, consisting of one part of wild honey, one part of terrestrial water and a third part of celestial water...the secret, the mystery was therefore in the vase." [20] It is reasonable to assume that the wild honey pertains to the lower third.

Surrounding the central circles of the Rose Windows in the North and South, where the Virgin is depicted as the throne of Christ, because he sits in her lap, in both cases there are 12 little circles between the central circle and the next circle. Inside these sub circles in both windows are fig leaves. The 1/3 portion that is associated with the third part, as it were, wild honey, is veiled in fig leaves.

The lower portion of the central circle in the South Rose window seems to act like a grail. It's invisible and situated below the breast of the Virgin and thusly becomes as a crucible from

---

[20] Etteila, Le Denier du Pauvre, in the Sept nuances de l'oevre philosophique, (1786), p 57. Extracted from Le Mystere des Cathedrales by Fulcanelli, 1922.

which milk flows and is held. Milk is white in color. Reflected in motif on the North Rose Window is Christ in his adult years holding a grail-ish chalice, though his life was arrested midway. When Christ was an infant he drank milk from the bosom of his Mother which is physical and a symbol of the apprentice. When Christ became a man, he drank milk from the grail, the Milk of his Mother; this is the spiritual interpretation and this spiritual milk is white. This may be compared with the white fruit of the Tree of Life that Lehi saw.

In the North Rose Window, the bottom half of the implied grail cup is situated such that per lore it would catch the blood and water of Christ from the wound in his side. Just as the Christ *child* drinks the milk of the *Love (LV)* of God, the latter-day adherent may drink from the cup of the sacrament. The sacrament in the restored church was originally wine. The color of wine is red. This represents partaking of the blood of the Son, which was shed for us, that we may have his spirit to be with us.[21] Interestingly the pelican is a white bird that will peck open its side to allow its young drink its blood. In this way the pelican has been used as a symbol of the Savior.

In contradistinction, we find that the two fruits on the trees in the Garden of Eden windows in Chartres Cathedral bear red fruit before the fall and white fruit after the fall. Before the fall, Adam and Eve appear almost as one being. Their lower portion almost appears as the four-legged torso of a horse or beast. After partaking of the fruit, they are tainted with red, yet the fruit of the tree is now represented as a white fruit. Interestingly, Adam and Eve are also now separate individuals. This division seems to imply that Adam and Eve have become like the gods, now

---

[21] D&C 20:79

having an individuality and agency to choose. We recall Adam and Eve adorn themselves with fig leaves after having partaken

XXVIII. Jehovah instructing Adam and Eve of the consequences of eating the fruit of the Tree of Knowledge of Good and Evil; note that Adam and Eve appear almost as one equine body undivided. Photo(s) by Dr. Stuart Whatling.

of the fruit to cover their procreative loins, they hadn't been aware of it before. But if there is a great and spacious building nearby with tourists pointing and mocking…I can imagine also pulling leaves off of a tree to cover myself. This lower third portion of our body and its association with wild honey is also found reflected above in the top third of the window, as the white fruit of the tree of life, or the philosopher's gold. That fall, or descension, was a necessary part of our progress.

Christ stood above a pavement of gold when he appeared above the breastwork in the temple in His visit to Joseph Smith and Oliver Cowdery. In The Revelation of John, John sees a city built on the foundation of 12 different stones upon which is built a city of gold. The city does not shine by the sun nor moon; for the Glory of God lights it. Since there are 12 signs of the zodiac, it seems that the wisdom sought of God of the symbols of

XXIX. After partaking the fruit now appears white; Adam and Eve are now divided by the tree.

the stars and their reflection on Earth gives necessary guidance and is often represented throughout time as a paved path of gold.

One may become curious to walk this path. To walk the path of the labyrinth is to walk the path of the Lord. Another representation of the path is to climb the *scala philosophurm*. These types of things suggest a godly walk, but being fallen how can it ever be so? As we have considered, the square pieces of the Incarnation Window at Chartres Cathedral appear as 9 rungs of a ladder. The 10th square, though incomplete is capped by the meeting of the two circles. Perhaps it may be said that the final step of ascension can only be made by *Way of the arc* or the Mercy of God. And so it is that we too, being incomplete are made complete and whole and may be brought into harmony with the divine law irrevocably decreed before the foundations of the heavens and earth by the atoning mercy of God. *So Mote it Be!*

Part II
Light Cleaveth Unto Light

Sir Isaac Newton and the Throne of Gravity

In the East Midlands of England there is a county called Lincolnshire. I've never been there. But in that county is a hamlet called Woolsthorpe-by-Colsterworth where there is a manor. On the 25th of December in the year 1642 there was born in this manor a baby and the name he was given was Isaac Newton. It's a well known story that Isaac Newton was sitting under an apple tree and an apple fell from the tree and hit him on the head. It is said that from this he formed his postulates on gravity and at last developed his 3 basic laws that govern the motion of bodies of mass. That's how the story typically goes. The incident was said to have occurred at home at the Woolsthorpe manor. From the time that he first told the story until the time of his death in 1727, he would apparently change the story and increase the elaboration to the point that people weren't sure if it really actually happened the way we now commonly hear the story. However, the physicist does not care if the origin story of the apple tree happened or not. The physicist takes the principles gleaned, uses them in the experiment of faith and becomes a smarter and happier physicist for it. I suppose some could reject Newton's laws of motion because there is enough suspiciousness about whether or not an apple actually fell on his head, such issues tempt the appetite of the iconoclast in spite of sensibility.

Let's reflect back on the scripture from Isaiah that says a branch grew out of the roots and a rod out of the stem of Jesse's tree. Let's imagine a rod growing out of the stem and draw upon some of the symbols gleaned from the contemplation of the Chartres symbolism. As we've discussed previously the rod is symbolized by a geometric line segment. When Lehi gains understanding of the Tree of Life and shares this with his sons, Nephi sets out to understand the symbols of the vision for himself. He learns that the iron rod represents the Word of God. Between Jesse and his posterity is the stem. The symbol of the iron rod grows out of the roots. The children are in the branches and the fathers are in the roots. Keeping them "at-one", though at a distance, is the attractive force of the iron rod. In the evening of Sept 21, 1823 the Angel Moroni informs Joseph Smith regarding the Angel Elijah that "He shall come to plant in the hearts of the children the promises made to the fathers, and the hearts of the children shall turn to their fathers." [1] This is an attractive force planted in the hearts of the children by the Spirit of Elijah, and thusly the seed of the iron rod is planted in the fruits. The very same message had been given to Malachi by the Lord with the warning that if this is not done, he will smite the earth with a curse. Smiting is done with a rod as well and so the iron rod has dual utilities. This consequence is further expressed in the words from the Angel Moroni to Joseph Smith that if it

---

[1] D&C 2:1

were not so, the *whole earth* would be utterly wasted at his coming." Sir Isaac Newton adds further insight into the symbolism the Lord uses in his treatise "Observations Upon The Prophecies of Daniel & The Apocalypse of St. John". Newton writes, "And because the whole kingdom is the body politic of the King, therefore the Sun, or a Tree, or a Beast, or Bird, or a Man whereby the King is Represented, is put in a large signification for the whole kingdom."[2] As the parts of Jesse's posterity are a part of Jesse, so also is the Kingdom the whole of the parts of the King. So, we glean from this that Isaac Newton sees the parts of the kingdom with respect to its whole under the governance and rule of the king. As demonstrated previously, the rule of the king is represented by the line segment extending from its center to the circumference of the circle and denotes the iron rod in its attractive forces or priesthood influence.

The book that Isaac Newton defines his laws of gravity in is called "The Principia: Mathematical Principles of Natural Philosophy" and was published in 1687. Newton's law of universal gravitation states, "Each mass particle attracts every other particle in the universe with a force that varies directly as the product of the two masses and inversely as the square of the distance between them."

$$F = -(GmM/r^2)e$$

Isaac Newton was leveraging the linear and square symbols found in the Tree of Jesse, whether aware of it or not, though I would imagine with intensive studies of the mathematical aspects

---

[2] Newton, Sir Isaac, "Observations Upon The Prophecies of Daniel & The Apocalypse of St. John", 1733. (reprint 2011 edition, Watchmaker Publishing, p.20)

of the Bible he would not have glanced over this. The axis of rotation of the whole earth is the rod that grows out of the stem. And the earth in its serpentine way rotates obediently around the axis. For this reason it is sometimes referred to as the *axis mundi*. We discussed previously, that the attractive properties make the iron and lodestone symbols nearly equivalent and are usually used in analogy equivalently.

In "The Principia" in Definition VIII, Newton humbly clarifies that he does not know the cause of the force of gravity, and thusly appeals to what the tree analogy would metaphorically suggest; the cause is lodestone.[3] However, Newton's results and observations are empirical and not meant to address the deeper "why" questions. Causality is not critical to the function of the equations he derived; even still this statement suggests he wrestled with the question. Ultimately he concedes that he doesn't know for sure if lodestone is at play.

"These quantities of forces, we may for brevity's sake, call by the names of motive, accelerative, and absolute forces; and, for distinction's sake consider them, with respect to the bodies that tend to the center; to the places of those bodies; and to the centre of force towards which they tend; that is to say, I refer to the motive force to the body as an endeavor and propensity of the whole towards the center, arising from the propensities of the several parts taken together; the accelerative force to the place of the body, as a certain power or energy diffused from the centre to all places around to move the bodies that are in them; and the absolute force to the centre, as endued with some cause, without which those motive forces would not be propagated

---

[3] Newton, Sir Isaac, "The Principia", 1588. (reprint edition 2010, Snowball Publishing, p. 12)

through the spaces round about; whether that cause be some central body (such as, in the center of the magnetic force, or the earth in the centre of the gravitating force) or anything else that does not yet appear. For I here design only to give a mathematical notion of those forces, without considering their physical causes and *seats*." [4]

Compare the concepts of the laws of attractive forces we have discussed here with what Joseph Smith reveals in D&C 88: 36-42 and consider Isaac Newton's use of the word *seats* in comparison with the use of the word *thrones* here. "All kingdoms have a law given; And there are many kingdoms; for there is no space in the which there is no kingdom; and there is no kingdom in which there is no space, either a greater or a lesser kingdom. And unto every kingdom is given a law; and unto every law there are certain bounds also and conditions. All beings who abide not in those conditions are not justified. For intelligence cleaveth unto intelligence; wisdom receiveth wisdom; truth embraceth truth; virtue loveth virtue; light cleaveth unto light; mercy hath compassion on mercy and claimeth her own; justice continueth its course and claimeth its own judgement goeth before the face of him who sitteth upon the *throne* and governeth all things."[5] The startling similarity more likely occurs because these symbols represent universally true and universally revealed archetypes and these archetypes are in the architecture of English thought. Though Isaac humbly leaves the central cause unnamed, the judgment seat he does refer to is discussed by the Lord to Joseph Smith in the Doctrine and Covenants. "He comprehendeth all things and all things are before him; and all things are round

---

[4]Newton, "The Principia", 1588. (reprint edition 2010, Snowball Publishing, p. 12)
[5] D&C 88:36-42

about him; and he is above all things, and is through all things, and is round about all things; and all things are by him, even God forever and ever. And again, verily I say unto you, he hath given a law unto all things, by which they move in their times and their seasons."[6]

The Plumb and Level

Walking into the entry to St. John's College on the Cambridge Campus you will see exhibited a plumb. A plum is a fruit, and a plumb is an architectural building tool used to identify the direction of gravitational force; they both dangle. The plumb is a tool of the mason. It also represents rectitude or a straight course leading to exaltation. The plumb represents the line connecting the earth to the Milky Way. The plumb and the level brought together may be symbolized by the square. The compass represents birth and the plumb and level, as the square represent both walking uprightly and being on the level with our brothers and sisters.

The Basque word *arana* means plum, and is associated with a valley. As we discussed earlier, *araigna* means spider and the thin thread is like the thin string that holds the plumb and denotes the direction of the force of gravity; the spiritual analog being a spiritual force of attraction.

---

[6] D&C 88:41

Intelligence Cleaveth Unto Intelligence [7]

I had visited France once before my visit to Chartres. I had spent about five days traveling with French sales reps in exotic locations such as Limoges, Nice, Bordeaux and finally ending up in Paris. It was on this trip that I also made the decision to throw out my khaki business pants and buy some French business dress pants, which is sort of my own French revolution. The only problem was that French guys must be pretty skinny. After my business meetings were done, I had two full days to explore Paris, while wearing my new pants. I had not yet come in contact with the person who had given to me the mysterious red book that I'd brought with me to Chartres, so at this point I knew very little of the information it contained. To have it on this day would have been priceless. Nonetheless, it was a late summer's day and I had no responsibilities other than to take it all in. My day in Paris would be astounding.

> *"Objects. Make it geometric,*
> *Make it rigid and then break it.*
> *Like a Coho, moving through liquid,*
> *Flow through and undulate*
> *And experience."*

I wrote this thought while walking through the busy streets of an autumn Paris; moving amongst the churning rivers of people and voices I felt my own calcified thinking within yearning to break apart, become malleable, calm and ready to

---

[7] D&C 88:39

take in whatever I might experience. Sycamore trees lined the streets and parks. Earlier that morning I'd gone to visit the Centre Pompidou modern art museum and experienced seeing the art of Picasso, Matisse, Kadinsky, Miro and the works of many others that I hadn't heard of. While I explored the different pieces of abstract art, I saw one that I would never have suspected would move me unless I saw it in the unexpected way that I did. In the middle of an exhibit room there was a pile of dirt, with broken up concrete sidewalk pieces on it. The soft life bearing soils had erupted through the rigidity of the manmade sidewalk. My own stubbornness of will felt like it was breaking up as I stared at the cracked pieces. I had compassion on the dirt. My mind understood what my heart needed. Without words, I felt it. One way or the other, the Earth, Nature, the Stars, the Galaxies and the Laws and Light that give them Life cannot be moved from their course. Likewise, there are parts of me that were designed exactly how the good Lord intended, and like that earth, the earth of my heart needed to come up. Nephi, the son of Helaman, says, "And the highways were broken up, and the level roads were spoiled and many smooth places made rough." The forces of nature and directives of Deity are ever in active perpetuity. If we find ourselves in harmony with these laws and in obedience to the Lord, we find ourselves free to act as agents of creation, but of even greater reward, we become ourselves. However, holding rigidly to any aspect of our will that is not in harmony with divine laws, we will experience what that sidewalk in the Centre Pompidou experienced. On this sunny warm Paris day to walk according to the softness of my heart, and move with the directive winds of divine orchestration, seemed to me to be a peaceful walk and perhaps at times, a godly walk. And so I let go of will, and strolled through the tree lined streets, along the

Seine River, to see and listen carefully to the words that this very old modern city might say to me. The wind on my fingertips gave my instinct its command.

In addition to this intriguing experiment of instinct I also needed to eat lunch. I decided to walk up to the roof top where there was a restaurant. As I walked up the industrially modeled open air corridor that traversed the side of the museum, I seemed to be one of only a few going up to the top. When I got to the top, the sun was just beginning its early afternoon traverse past the noon hour and lit up Paris so that its irradiance was elegantly brilliant. On the museum rooftop there was a very nice looking restaurant with small tables out. I went to look at a menu only to find that the prices were a bit high for my budget and I preferred to keep moving and seeing anyway. But for this small time I would take in everything I could. As I walked back towards the viewing point to the West, I passed a few tables. On each table was a slim vase. In each vase was a tall red rose.

I looked out over Paris and could see the Eiffel tower and parts of the Seine River. I tried to take photos but my camera batteries ran out. So I did what I always do when my camera batteries run out. I recall that with surety every bit of info we see, hear, smell, taste and touch is recorded somewhere in the libraries of our mind and can be recalled later, then I stare at what I want a picture of and just look until it sears onto my memory. And so it is there. It is in my mind.

I can imagine looking down on the streets as if I were still there. Since then I have read more of the history of Paris. Times were not always so peaceful. I thank God for the beauty that has blossomed since then; though even in those darker times there were those things that were a light, things that were praiseworthy, things of good report. Though, good report would have to be discrete, quiet report was safe report and if not conveyed with caution, the report could end in a noose or later in a guillotine. The woman had fled in to the wilderness where she hath a place prepared of God, that they should feed her there a thousand two hundred and threescore years. Could she have been here? Some say so. She brought forth a man child who was to rule all nations with a rod of iron; and her child was caught up unto God and his throne. In the summer of 1623, something happened one day. Like waking up in the morning to find dews had settled out in the night, something distilled out of obscurity. All over the walls of Paris appeared a poster:

"We the Deputies of the Higher College of the Rose-Croix, do make our stay, visibly and invisibly, in this city, by the Grace of the Most High, to Whom turn the hearts of the Just. We demonstrate and instruct, without books and distinctions, the ability to speak all manners of tongues of the countries where we choose to be, in order to draw our fellow creatures from the error of death.

He who takes it upon himself to see us merely out of curiosity will never make contact with us. But if his inclination seriously impels him to register in our fellowship, we, who are judges of intentions, will cause him to see the truth of our promises; To the extent that we shall not make known the place of our meeting in this city, since the thoughts attached to the real desire of the seeker will lead us to him and him to us."[8]

---

[8] Manifesto poster posted in Paris in 1623

I can just imagine the electricity in the air the morning that people on the streets of Paris read this manifesto; jumpstarting hope in the hearts of those looking for a greater era of truth and light and an end to despotism, yet those that posted this message were wisely veiled from plain site.

This manifesto was announced precisely 1260 years after the Nicene Creed began to be effectuated under the Antiochene Synod of 363 A.D. It was also announced at a time when pilgrims would begin to cross the ocean to America in search of a new beginning.

The principle that the manifesto makes clear is that the seeker of truth will find the seeker of truth. It is a universal principal. Intelligence cleaveth unto intelligence and light cleaveth unto light. Without compulsory means, seekers of truth may be led to each other so that light and intelligence may be exchanged or as sometimes called, edified. Edify means to build up. The principle of attraction is one of the primary functions of the iron rod; action at a distance. As we discussed earlier, the iron rod may be represented geometrically as a line segment.

A New Axial Time in Geometric Symbolism

The singularity of the manifesto of 1623 in Paris seems to identify this event as a significant date in the Divine Plan. Thusly we can prepare to represent events around this event in geometric symbolism and we will identify related events that are pertinent to the cycle. We will plan to use the basic geometry of the Chartres Labyrinth; the radius and the circle. We will represent a timeline by drawing a radius from center to circumference, circumscribing a circle with a compass, then with a straight edge draw the line segment returning back to the center. Imagine truth radiating and propagating like light from a point source, veiled from the eyes of the world. The point source is the origin in the "center of centers". In this case, imagine that at the origin is an ark of the covenant or also a body organized and unbroken. The circle represents the furthermost circumference from the center of a kingdom, it's outer edges are as the edge of the forest. In polar coordinates this would define a "domain" (ד). So, the small box carrying truth, priesthood, authority, order or bodily organization is moved from the center to the furthest boundary, which boundary is set by the Lord. It endures an entire lifecycle, thereby going a full round. At the further circumference, that order of the body is scattered into its parts, each part as a cog on a gear. Order at the outer boundary is the least orderly that the Lord will permit. Consider imaginatively the Ark of the Covenant traveling around this circle, azimuthally along the circumference until it completes a full cycle. When it has completed its cycle, it returns to the kingdom, to the center of centers. On its journey back to the center and its return to unity, its brokenness mends and its being increases in order, leaving the wilderness as it makes its return to the center of the kingdom. The center is a point, a symbol of unity and oneness. The attributes of being scattered and reunited are symbolized in the scattering and gathering of the tribes of Israel as well as the scattering and resurrection of the body parts of Osiris. It would seem that the authority of God on Earth is similar. Perhaps represented here also is the "word" associated with the priesthood which continueth in the church of God in all generations and is without beginning of days or end of years.[9] After the body parts of Osiris were scattered upon the face of the land by Set, Isis, the mother of Horus, gathered in the parts of her beloved husband, yet she kept one key part for herself. She kept the phallus. As we discovered in a contemplation of the Tree of Jesse, the phallus in this type of case represents masculine power, logos, rectitude, the iron rod and the word of God. The church or the woman that fled into the wilderness may be considered to be the scattered Israel or the church (*cyrcle*) of God and holds within it the iron rod. This is a thought experiment and may only have the measure of validity we want to give it, but if it works it will be fruitful in revealing some new truth. That's a pretty good gage of its usefulness as a device for gaining more understanding.

While the rolling forth of St. John the Revelator's 1260 year cycle where the "word" is enwombed in gestation within a circle proceeds, there is simultaneously another lifecycle rolling forth according to the great gears of heavenly providence. Sometime around 400-421 A.D., gold metal plates of the sons of Lehi are buried in a stone box safely guarded by a grove of trees within the hill known as Cumorah in upstate York. They aren't in the old York, but rather the New York; the one in the colonies not far from where the French would battle the British in an effort to secure the land to the subjection of their throne. Divine Providence would favor the British and the land round about the hill Cumorah would go to the British and with it any stone boxes contained therein. The voices of the sons of Lehi are beginning

---

[9] D&C 84:17

to speak as a voice from the dust as one that hath a familiar spirit. The gold plates exude the call of the voices.

The 1260 year period from the Antiochene Synod 163 A.D. to the Manifesto of the Rose-Croix may be taken to be a full cycle 'time' and we will represent it as the circle. The radius of a 1260 year circle is 200.15 years. Add 200.15 years to the summer of 1623 A.D. and we arrive at autumn of 1823. On September 21-22 of 1823, Joseph Smith Jr. received the first visits by the Angel Moroni. This period is the period of "return". We may use 163 A.D. as a viable point of origin for the radius that resembles "fleeing" into the wilderness, or the beginning of a generalized apostasy. 163 A.D. is also the first tetrad year[10] that occurs on Passover since the time of Christ. So what is a tetrad? A tetrad is a series of four lunar eclipses or *blood red moons* over a relatively short period of time. This initiates an era of persecution against men and women of faith and reason and against the true followers of Jesus. Persecutions raged against men and women such as St. Justin who taught that the seeds of Christianity predated the birth of Jesus the Christ in preparation of his coming and held to a doctrine of "seed bearing word" (*logos spermatikos*); he tended towards a Platonic-Christianity. Thusly, from 163 A.D. to 363 A.D. the timeline as drawn geometrically travels from the center origin along a straight line away from the center. The next period is from 363 A.D. until 1623 A.D. and traces the circumference of the circle. It is during this period that "the woman is in the wilderness", the word of God alive, yet the body is scattered; matter unorganized coupled with potential energy and prophecy of return. 1623 A.D.

---

[10] National Aeronautics and Space Administration Catalog of Lunar Eclipses: 101CE - 200 CE

reasonably marks the time when the woman begins to come out of the wilderness. The final period is a return from the circumference of the 1260 year circle back to the center of the circle in a straight and narrow course to the center of centers which is the origin or "seed" location of our geometric symbol. This period of time from 1623 A.D. to 1823 A.D. is the period of time from the Rose-Croix manifesto to the time when the Angel Moroni visits Joseph to commission him to find and translate the gold plates. This too can be expressed as a line segment from the outer circumference to the center. It represents the "word of God" being planted as a seed in preparation for the restoration of the "fulness of times"; the golden dawning of a restoration of the Priesthood.

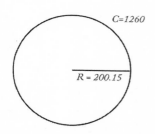

XXX. *One possible 1260 year circle with 200.15 year radius.*

The circle, though representative in time of a cycle also represents the unity of all truth. The length of the radius establishes the area in the circle; the magnitude of truth revealed. So the geometric symbol may represent both a timeline cycle and it may represent a pattern of God's method for working with His children.

Louis Claude de Saint Martin (b. 1743 A.D. - d. 1803 A.D.) writes about his views of the Creator relying heavily on geometric symbolism as a teaching device:

> "The Eternal, all-powerful Creator, whose infinite power extends through the Universe of spirits and bodies, contains within its immensity countless numbers of beings which it emanates from its bosom as it pleases. It gives to each of

these beings laws, precepts, and commandments, which serve as points of connection between the different beings and this Great Divinity.

The connection between all these beings with the Being is so absolute, that no effort by these beings can prevent it. Whatever they do, they can never come out of the circle they have been placed in, and each point of the circle that they travel over could never for a moment cease being in bond, communication and connection with the *center of centers.*

The connection of individual centers with the Universal is the Holy Spirit. The connection of the universal center with the center of center of centers is the Son; and the center of centers is the all powerful Creator. In this way, God the Father creates beings, His son gives them life, and this life is the Holy Spirit."[11]

St. Martin identifies here in essence what Joseph Smith Jr. identifies in his interpretation of The Book of Abraham Facsimile 2. There is a divine connection within our Father in Heaven. When we become more unified with God, we become more unified with each other. Yet there is always individuality and agency. The Lord, speaking through Joseph Smith, says, "All truth is independent in that *sphere* in which God has placed it, to act for itself, as all intelligence also; otherwise there is no existence. Behold here is the agency of man."[12] With our God-given agency is the liberty to choose the right or wrong; yet resurrection and the path of redemption are wrought by the

---

[11] Louis Claude de Saint-Martin, "The Man of Desire" (L'homme de desir), 1790.
[12] D&C 93:30

atonement of Christ that through faith and repentance and the spiritual progression that accompanies that process we may return to the presence of the Father. Both limb and joint shall be restored; everything shall be restored to its perfect frame.[13]

Consider that the symbol that we use to model the apostasy cycle is also in the likeness of the labyrinth symbol. As we think about the story of Theseus, we may see that the literal history of western man from 163 A.D. to 1823 A.D. is akin to the entire human race following the hero's journey of Theseus in overcoming the trials of the circular labyrinth or we may duly consider it to be the journey of Adam and Eve in their ascension from out of a dark and dreary world to begin the return to the Tree of Life.

It is through the many success stories of intelligence cleaving unto intelligence and light cleaving unto light that brought about the Age of Enlightenment and laid the foundation to bring the church out of obscurity in the last days and introduced us to a new age of vitality.

---

[13] Alma 11:40-45

Part III
Rivers of Light

Rock Creek

There is, in the community of fly fishermen with whom I associate, a retired English professor, or perhaps I should say a retired American professor that taught English. His wit is as sharp as his hooks are bent. His name is Harry and let it be noted that he invented the coffee-bean fly pattern. Harry noticed that while most trout streams in Northern California have unique names like Hat Creek, Pit River, McCloud or the Sacramento River, there are many creeks that share the common name of "Rock Creek". On the west slope of the Northern Sierra Nevada mountain range, several creeks feed into the North Fork of the Feather River, yet locals may refer to any of several of these feeder creeks as Rock Creek. Harry joked that there is really only one Rock Creek. It flows underground and then emerges to flow above ground for a while in one location, flows back underground and then pops up somewhere else to flow a bit. The Rock Creek in Montana is the same Rock Creek that flows near Mammoth California on the Southern East Slope and so on. Though it is the musing joke of an old-timer fly fisherman that all Rock Creeks are really the one and the same Rock Creek, as we cast our minds to the spiritual rivers where archetypes reveal the flows and emanations of intelligence from the eternal spring of the Divine Center, it may be worthwhile to consider how it is that these Rock Creeks flow. In fact, if there is a creek somewhere that doesn't yet have a name, then it is probably Rock Creek too.

Regarding underground stream-flow, it is a fact of hydrology that some streams flow through a drainage basin in full flow in spring with the sounds of rushing white waters, yet in late summer and in fall the stream may only flow underground in divided rivulets through flat sedimentary stretches unseen to fish or fisher, only to reappear above ground further down the drainage basin. Populations of trout may still live in the cold small pools that remain though as a small trickle through the fall season. When the winter rains come, the river swells and the fish may move freely through the stream. This may happen every year to the stream and so the cycle goes on. Seasoned fly fishermen are well acquainted with the seasons of the stream as also are the fishers of men.

In the book called "The First Book of Adam and Eve", a river flows from the roots of the Tree of Life, conveying the idea that all things flow from a common origin. Traditions, genetic traits, language, cultural strengths and weaknesses, prosperity and destitution all may flow from parents to children and from generation to generation. I like to think the magic that germinates English poetry also flows from the roots of words as well. Whatever one chooses to call it, the life blood that is intelligence seems to have a life of its own. The fly fisherman and author, Norman Maclean, says it well, "Eventually, all things merge into one, and a river runs through it. The river was cut by the world's great flood and runs over rocks from the basement of time. On some of the rocks are timeless raindrops. Under the rocks are the words, and some of the words are theirs. I am haunted by waters." There are three rivers shared between the human family and the heavens and earth themselves, that seem to carry nutrition and wisdom to the spiritual angler; namely etymology, number and geometry.

A River Called Etymology

"Poetry is when emotion has found its thought and thought has found words."

–Robert Frost

In both Hebrew and Egyptian traditions of old, the power of words were well recognized and given much reverence. Christ too treated words with reverence for when he was presented with paradox or peril, he afforded himself the time he needed to formulate what he wanted to say and precisely how he wanted to say it. It was by the *Word* of God that the Lord's creations assumed order. Jehovah effectuated the creation process through his angelic workforce. There are, flowing like waters through the languages of the ancient world to the present, streams of thought and meanings that left the hand of the originators thousands of years ago and have flowed to our times. There is a spiritual power encapsulated in these ancient roots of words. They are carriers of spiritual light. The lover of words may drop the plume to paper, and in the creative process of writing find there is a life that springs forth from the roots of words and blossoms into manifold meanings. Sometimes, in the casting of rhyme or prose, a meaning rises to the surface, sometimes to behold and sometimes to belay, sometimes to release or employ another day. Whether intentional or not, when held loosely, like beholding the wings of a butterfly as it rests in the open palm of one's hand, a word carries its own power and vitality beyond the limited view of the writer that attempts to capture meaning. Etymology is the study of the flow of meaning through the roots of words as the currents of time take them from one language to the next, one culture to the next and one epoch to another.

Many of the roots of words that we commonly use from day to day can be traced back to ancient times to the most primal symbols. The letters themselves tell a story and are deeply embedded in the roots of both mankind and the roots of words themselves. A bull's head, a fire, a cave, a mother's breast, a spiral swirl, phallic symbols or a tree are some of the symbols we use freely everyday in worded messages in our work, on television commercials, road signs and in church without ever seeing past the modern semantics and into their older meanings. I would posit that at some primal level the symbols whisper the ancient word to us in spite of our unawareness. The most basic letters seem to indicate things that have to do with our most basic physiological and safety needs. The letter A as a symbol descends from the head of the Taurus or bull or *apis*; as such, it may represent the power to pull a plough and till and aerate the earth to prepare to plant seeds. It also looks like the water level line midway up Mount Ararat where Noah's boat docked. In this way it may represent a mountain top from which there is safety from floods, and from where the beginning of the next axial time may begin. It also appears to be birthing a horizontal line segment. Tipped on its side, it looks like an open mouth. Interestingly in sound physics it is the length defined by two nodes fastening a cord that defines the frequency of the sound that will ripple into the air when plucked. That little line segment in the A inherently represents sound like when we open our mouth and make a sound. The Egyptian symbol for *the creative word* is a mouth with three jots below which give it the enumeration of 1/3. From this same letter A, the Tree of Jesse takes form. Imagine the horizontal line being re-engineered to the bottom of the letter A and its length growing to continue to make at-one that distance between the two legs of the A. As it hits the ground, imagine it assumes the form of Jesse horizontally lying on his couch in the Chartres Jesse Window. This is akin to the rod of Jesse. Out of the rod grows a stem. This is the vertical line at 90 degrees to the rod. This forms the letter T or the tau from Taurus. The Egyptian temple goer would bring a tau symbol to their lips, as a symbol of initiation. The letter A also is the first letter in *Alpha*. Christ is the Alpha and Omega, the beginning and the end; He atoned for the sins of mankind and died on the cross, which may be represented by the tau.

These three examples show correspondence between the primal symbolic meanings of the letters themselves. Again, they mostly relate to the basics of human physiological needs and security needs. Interestingly however, those same needs are typical or a reflection of our spiritual needs. The letter C is the first letter of cave. It is also the first letter in concave. The geometry of the letter C itself looks in essence like a cave. In Hebrew, the letter "ב" is Beth. *Beth* tends to have the same cavernous appearance of a roof over a floor, like the manger in Jerusalem (*Beth*lehem) that Jesus was born in. If there were a neighborhood of letters and it started to rain and you had to choose a letter as a shelter from the rain, you might choose to get into the letter C if you are in Europe or if you are visiting the suburbs of Jerusalem you might find a good looking letter like ב to get under. If it gets windy though, you might look around for something warmer, something with a door like the letter D. The letter D looks like a backwards C with a line for a door enclosing the warmth of the C in. The letter D is also the first letter of the word "Door". In Hebrew the letter called Daleth is "ד", which is traditionally cited as being a roof with a tent flap hanging down; door or portal. *De* or *d'* placed before a noun meaning "of" that thing, has a similar meaning as being the fruit of something, or having exited as through a door from; being born of it or into it. 'Dios' would be the "door of the o's" or "door of the circles". The French "d'or" meaning "of gold"...or very cleverly found in the name of the female hero, *Dorothy*, who begins her journey to the Land of Oz by leaving the from the center of a golden spiral. ד is a good letter to represent the entrance to the labyrinth at Chartres Cathedral.

The letter "F" looks like a funny tree with two branches coming out on the right side; the higher up one and the smaller younger branch below. "F" is interesting in that we talk about how the Hebrews considered the name of God to be "ineffable". It's like half a capital T and half a lower case t in one. Well, the closest relative in Hebrew is the letter "פ", which looks like an open mouth or a tree branch with a dangling fruit ready to fall. It is pronounced similar to a "peh" P or PF. It is associated with the meaning "mouth". As if that dangling piece is being eaten at the same time. So, when we hear that the Hebrews used Tetragrammaton to symbolically represent the "ineffable" name of God, we will finded embedded in the English roots of the word "ineffable" we are using a spelling of the letter "eff". "Ineffable" then behaves something like the "not mouthable" word of God. The branches of the letter F may also bear fruit. "Fruit" starts with the letter F. And this is how it goes.

So the next time you drive past "Casa De Fruta" you may want to stop in to get out of the rain, close the door behind you and enjoy putting some fruit in your mouth. If you are getting off of work in silicon valley and text your date to let him or her know to meet you at CDF and your date gets the essence of what you are saying he or she will meet you at Casa De Fruta. However, if he or she sees it another way, they may try to meet you at the California Department of Forestry, so either more letters are necessary or you may need to find a new date with a weirder and more eccentric sense of humor.

It seems apparent that "the letter of the law" has to do with the exasperating yet exacting details of the letter symbols. When Alma of the Book of Mormon teaches that Christ will fulfill the Law of Moses, every jot and every tittle; he is describing the completeness with which the atonement fulfils all of the required demands of justice; tending to the furthermost wisps of the infinitesimally small, yet requisite details of the law. In this English metaphor, the tittle is the part of a letter that requires a tiny nuance in the writing of the letter; a slight swoosh. The two Hebrew letters Kaph and Beth are nearly indistinguishable to the modern American eye, the differentiating feature being the tittle. Kaph is כ and ב is Beth. The tittle is known as a diacritic. The Latin tilde is a squiggly wavy line ~. Unlike the undulations of the tittle and tilde, the paths of the Lord are straight. Filling the law, every jot and tittle, seems to mean compensating for every deviation from the straight line or irrevocably decreed law. Given a fairly straight tree trunk, the tilde and tittle are the snaky windings of life that give a tree its twists, the bends and burls that differentiate a tree trunk from a lamp post. The letter with the most extreme tittle is the letter S as in 'snake' or as found in the dollar sign symbol, $, which looks like a snake in a helical hold around a pillar or rod. Human DNA, the code of life itself, is helical in nature like the snake. To allow ourselves to be born is to submit ourselves to a serpentinely cyclical but finite existence in the temporal plane. The sin wave in trigonometry is snaky and so is its mate, the cosine. Venturing to decant the meaning from one set of words to the vessel of another, we might soberly say, when the sins of the male angels and the sins of the female angels are justified, paid for through the atonement of the Savior, and their paths made straight, they are then prepared to be married and sealed as one. They surpass the potential of angels and come closer to being like Elohim, gods both male and female. This richly symbolic *versum viridem* may be expressed as unity in mathematical symbols as sin squared plus cosine *squared*:

$$\sin{}^2 + \cos{}^2 = 1.$$

The apprentice pillar at Roslyn chapel has a helical floral pattern coiling up and around the outside of the pillar. In total there are four helices growing out of the base of what would otherwise be square in appearance. However, the master pillar has a square cross section; it has no helical spirals and is thusly without the aforementioned tittle.

So what about the jot? The jot of the law? Well, it rhymes with dot which must count for something. Like the dot on the Latin letter "i". In the Latin derivative language Spanish, "jot" is the root word of *jota* which means the letter "j". J is for justice but also for Jachin. A close representation in Hebrew is Tzaddi

"צ", as in Tzedek, which is the last part of the name Melchizedek. Justice without mercy is severity. Just as the severity of the letter of the law killeth (2 Cor 3:6), so also when the tip of the sword is brought to the breast, it will make a painful point. The "j" also looks like a fish hook. Hebrew Tzaddi as a final letter gematrically enumerates to 104 and means "fish hook" when spelled out: צדי. The enumeration as a final ץ is 900. Noah lived to be 900 and 50. The number 50 as an alpha or beginning letter means "fish". So Noah's age of 900 and 50 may be given the meaning of "fish hook" and "fish". When the justice of God was poured out on the face of the whole Earth in the times of Noah, it was done to fulfill the laws of justice, every jot and tittle, as it was the baptism of the Earth. When the law was fulfilled and all were destroyed but 8, the waters receded and the Earth consumed those that were not justified. So, fishhook and fish are symbols of a similar meaning as the jot and tittle. More importantly, however, the meanings lead us to consider the alpha and omega characteristics of fish and fish hook. Just as the serpent with the lion head circles around and eats the end of its tail, the fish bites the hook and is taken from the water. Noah was not caught by the severity of the law. Jesus, the master fisher of men taught, "Be ye therefore merciful that ye might receive mercy." Noah was sustained by the elements and carried to safety by mercy; this ended one axial time and began the next.

Let's take a closer look at a common word that carries many meanings and operates to transform word to number to principle in an amazing way. This electrifying word to consider is *arc*. Arc is built of just three letters that seem to be quite busy and play a critical roll in carrying the continuity that nails together one axial time to the next; and for starters, "arc" could reasonably stand for "A Royal Cave". In the context of geometry, an arc is a finite curve segment that is part of a circle. Two rays extending from the center of curvature of the arc that meet the ends of the curve segment subtend the arc angle. So the word "arc" plays a lead role in geometry and is almost always associated with angles. Arc and angle have a playful nature and may emerge in a kindred meaning as arch and angel. The geometry of an architectural arch is an arc. Moses' ark contained the 10 commandments on two tablets. It is described as having 2 cherubim that act like a Urim and Thummim, where God would meet Moses to speak with him. (Exodus 25:22) In the case of the Urim and Thummim, Joseph Smith described two stones being placed in two bows. Bows really are a lot like arcs. That sounds speculative at first, but then consider that the Latin word for bow is *arcus*. In fact, another type of arc is found in the Book of Abraham, Facsimile 2, fig. 2 where there is a stone being brought down from outside of the arc of the hypocephalus circle, into the circle attached to what looks like two arcs or bows between the horns of the minotauresque looking symbol for Olibish. Arc is also found being carried within the Latin word *barca,* which means barge or boat. A vessel for carrying people, such as Noah's Ark is found in Abr. Facs. 2, fig. 3.

Since an arc is subtended in geometry by its corresponding arc angle, let's now consider the word angle. We can then begin to see, as an example, how fishing terms, angle and rod are connected to the word "arc" and thusly how words we use every day are carriers of ancient and profoundly deep meanings. It serves us to accept the semantics that modernly don the body of the ancient words; though it is an endeavoring in seeing beyond the mist to discover ancient meanings reincarnate deep within the marrow of modern language. Let's explore this. Angle is a very Englishy word because the name England itself derives from the word "angle". Anciently, migrants to England came from the North from the land of the Angle. Fly fishing evolved in England and is called angling. Fly fishermen may be called anglers. When casting a dry fly, I am circumscribing in the sky above an arc with the fly rod and my hand and forearm are the motive *power* behind the angle. What roll does the *rod* play in angling? "Rod" and "root" are of common meaning as we see in the Tree of Jesse symbolism. The English rod, root, Latin *rota*, ray, radius, right and German *recht* and Hebrew resh ר all hail from a common family tree. The Latin word, *Rex*, while sounding like Germen 'recht' meaning right or correct, means royal. 'Root' is akin to the Latin for wheel, rota, and thus carries the imagery of the spokes of the wheel as the radius rotating around the axis. The Old English word *rodd* is a slender stick or shoot coming forth from a tree. We can then complete the connection by finding the description of how to build a fly fishing rod in "A treatyse of fysshynge wyth an Angle" written by Dame Juliana Berners in 1496. In the relatively short writing she explains how to build a fly rod by cutting a long stick from a willow or asp tree. In this case, she refers to the rod as a "staffe". This is done at the time of year between the two celebrations known as Michaelmas and Candlemas, which were celebrated on September 29 and February 2 respectively. She writes, "And howe you shall make your rod craftely, here I shall teache you, ye shall cut betweene Michelmas & Candelmas a fayre staffe of a fadome and a halfe longe and arme great of hasyll, wyllowe or aspe, and breath hym in a hote ouen, and set hym euen." At the ends of the rod she instructs to attach iron eye hole, "Then shaue your staffe and make hym capre waye, then vyrell the staffe at both endes with long hoopes of yron or larton, in the clennest wyse, a pyke in the nether ende fastened with a rennyng vyce, to take in and out your crop."[1]

It is by the "staffe" or "rodd" of the willow or asp tree that the angler may build a rod to catch a fish. Dame Juliana Berners then explains how to make 12 flies, one for each month of the year. Thusly each of the twelve months the fly fisherman angles a different fly pattern, acknowledging the change in appetite of the fish as the seasons change. "Simon Peter saith unto them, I go a fishing. They say unto him, We also go with thee. They went forth and entered into a ship immediately and that night they caught nothing." They had not yet the iron rod or the word of their God amongst their fishing crew. Later then, the Master Fisherman, Jesus instructs his new crew where to cast their nets, "Cast the net on the *right* side of the ship, and ye shall find. They cast therefore, and now they were not able to draw it for the multitude of fishes." [2]

---

[1] Dame Juliana Berners, "A treatyse of fysshynge wyth an Angle", 1486.
[2] John 21:6

A River Called Gematria

*"The Secret Doctrine is the common property of
countless millions of men born under various
climates, in time with which history refuses to deal,
and to which esoteric teachings assign dates
incompatible with the theories of Geology and
Anthropology."*

–Helena P. Blavatsky

So did Noah live to be 950 years old or was the number 950 a teaching device? Or was it both? Were exceptionally different calendar systems used in the time of Noah or were life spans actually different?

When I was a young man, my bishop called me to be a counselor in the Priest's Quorum presidency in the 16-18 year old boys group at church. We had a planning meeting in the living room at his house to plan a big activity for the boys to go on that coming summer. He taught us about the creative process of brainstorming that could be used for coming up with new ideas we'd never before considered. He drew a picture of a stick person, a wall-like barrier and some figure representing a solution or epiphany on the other side of the barrier. He told us young men that this drawing is like the thinking process going on in the mind. He taught us that sometimes to get around a barrier we need to use our creativity and that it is like going under water to go under the barrier and then we come out on the other side with some new ideas. I was intrigued but barely got the depth of what he was saying at the time. Regardless, somehow or other we managed to plan a trip to the Colorado River in Havasupi Canyon. Well, over the years I began to practice and observe what he was talking about. That lesson stuck with me. I later learned in college as I worked to improve my study habits and thinking devices that there is some active mechanism or perhaps some internal metaphoric angler of dream symbols that looks for answers in the waters of our subconscious; something beyond our own awareness that seeks out, gathers and assimilates information. Sometimes we have to let go of our objective reasoning and yield our best thinking up to the Lord until the Lord returns to us an answer. In the story of the Brother of Jared, the man called "The Brother of Jared", is leading his people after the confounding of tongues at the tower of Babel to flee to a far away land. It is recorded in the Book of Mormon that those people eventually arrive in the Americas. They built barges of some sort, but they could think of no way to light their barges to cross the formidable sea. The barges were sealed tight like unto a dish and closed on the top. So, the Brother of Jared does all he can; he brings stones to the Lord. The Lord, from beyond the veil, extends his hand through the veil to touch the stones and the stones light up. While I've never known anyone to have that particular experience in a strictly literal sense, there is a workable analogy here. When we have worked hard to piece together the parts that we understand to a problem and we are stuck, we can take our incomplete work, after all we can do, to the Lord at which point he will light the way. The best *prima materia* we have, when given to the Lord, can be enough to allow him to enlighten our minds when we need to traverse waters to a new land; whether they be the waters of creation, creativity or personal guidance.

As we strive to make sense of things that seem irreconcilable in our spiritual progress, sometimes a way presents itself. Typically in our day and age numbers are fixed values that represent some measure that is given units. Units describe the properties being measured. Typical units are for example: meters to measure distance, liters to measure volume, years, days, hours, seconds to measure time or nanometers to measure light wavelength or ohms to measure resistance. Anciently and up to this very day in some modern works too, authors use a peculiar literary device that is based on a number system that operates independently of units of measure. It's hard to grasp at first, so don't grasp too hard. In fact, hold on loosely. In life, we start life by counting objects like fingers. If we counted to five, the units were fingers. If we counted apples, the units were apples. It's hard to imagine numbers without some sort of units; our minds expect units to be associated with numbers. However, numerical symbols themselves carry qualitative meaning. Similarly, an algebraic variable may represent many things. The number symbol may in fact be associated with a letter or a meaning. The Hebrew lettering system was developed so that a letter has a corresponding number. This system is commonly referred to as gematria.

Before talking about the specifics of gematria, it's good to understand some history of numbers and mathematical thinking that will then make this literary device more reasonable, to some degree. In the book of 2 Nephi 2:11 Lehi teaches that all things must needs be a compound in one. This is reflective of the mathematics of his time 600 years B.C. The number 0 wasn't invented or assimilated into mathematical thinking until several centuries A.D. Before that time, Egyptians, Persians and Hebrews relied on the concept of unity. All things are a compound in one. This means that 1 + (-1) doesn't equal zero, but rather it means that one thing was somewhere and then it got moved to somewhere else. The concept of the Law of Conservation of Mass is a modern law of physics and is good example of this thinking being applied. Something could approach an infinitesimally small ratio of something else, but as it gets smaller, its brother and sister parts are being scattered somewhere else. It is a very reasonable model of thinking and we use it in physics all of the time really. It just says that all things are interconnected.

Gematria is an identification system that guides its interpreter through a numerical mapping of literarily corresponding meanings. It allows two symbols to mate in an arranged marriage of meanings and beget new meanings. It fits in to the process described by my bishop as a young man in that it facilitates the immersion of the mind into the waters of creative thinking in order to discover new views, ideas and creative possibilities! All things are a compound in one, so let's see how the parts are interconnected! What is amazing is that it seems to have been employed by authors of ancient scripture. How it got there I do not know, but like Rock Creek it flows through the scriptures here and there surfacing at times to perplex the eye of reason and then seeps back underground to flow under the rocks. Beneath the story, beyond the procession of time, built by eternal architects there is a skeletal structure around which the vitality of life takes form. Life itself insinuates that structure. A zen adage says that the longer you look at something, the more you see what is really there.

Hebrew–English Gematria Equivalents

English Letter	Hebrew Letter	Hebrew Letter Pronunciation in Common English	Number
A	א or ע	Aleph or Ayin	1 or 70
B	ב	Beth	2
C (hard)	כ or ק	Kaph or Qoph	20 or 100
C (soft)	ס	Samekh	60
Ch	ח	Cheth	8
D	ד	Daleth	4
E	ה	Heh	5
F	ו or פ	Vau or Peh	6 or 80
G	ג	Gimel	3
H	ה	Heh	5
I	י	Yod	10
J	י	Yod	10
K	כ or ק	Kaph or Qoph	20 or 100
K final	ך	Kaph final	500
L	ל	Lamed	30
M	מ	Mem	40
M final	ם	Mem final	600
N	נ	Nun	50
N final	ן	Nun final	700
O	ע or ו	Ayin or Vau	70 or 6
P	פ	Peh	80
P final	ף	Peh final	800

Q	ק	Qoph or Kaph	100 or 20
R	ר	Resh	200
S	ס	Samekh	60
Sh	ש	Shin	300
T	ט	Teth	9
Th	ת	Tau	400
Tz	צ	Tzaddi	90
Tz final	ץ	Tzaddi final	900
U	ו	Vau	6
V	ו	Vau	6
W	ו	Vau	6
X	צ or ח	Tzaddi or Cheth	90 or 8
Y	י	Yod	10
Z	ז	Zain	7

So, let's return to take a look at the word "ARC" through the lens of gematria and find out what may come of it. Using the chart of number equivalents to English and Hebrew letters[1], let's sum all the possible enumerations of the English letters A, R and C. We find there are four possible numbers: 222, 301, 290 and 370. We could likely explore each one and discover something interesting. In this case, let's choose 370 because it's close to the number of days in a year. 370 is enumerated by using the Hebrew letters Ayin ע (70) + Resh ר (200) and Qoph ק (100) = 370. The first letters of Ayin, Resh and Qoph would be more like ARQ as in *barq*, which is Persian for lightning or *barque*

---

[1] Lon Milo Duquette, "The Chicken Qabalah of Rabbi Lamed Ben Clifford", 2001, Weiser Books.

which is middle French meaning a ship or barge. Geometrically, 2π is 360 deg and 370 is conspicuously close to that considering it came from the word "arc" to begin with. So, are there any arc stories in the canon of Hebrew scriptures where 370 arises? Yes, indeed! Noah entered the "ark", in "the six hundredth year of Noah's life, in the second month, the seventeenth day of the month". That's a fortuitous discovery! Further exploration reveals that 600 is the equivalent of the Hebrew letter Mem, which letter represents water. "It was in the six hundredth and first year...in the second month on the twenty and seventh day of the month, was the earth dried" and Noah and each of the 8 souls got off of the ark and were saved. Noah and his family and crew were on board the ark for 370 days! The gematria meaning of 370 is mathematically unitless. So the word "Arc" not only enumerates to imply a ship or barge but, also, as a geometric symbol represents a concept; it is a form of "things that act" and related to motive power. When the units of days are given to be 370, the form of "arc" as "the power to move" or "things that act" is then fixed to a temporal meaning that we can more easily relate to. However, "arc" itself here may be taken as an "archetype". Furthermore, it is no surprise that as a form of "the power to move", there are winged cherubim adorning the arc of the covenant that Moses received; recalling that Joseph Smith had clarified that winged beasts are symbolic of the "power to move".

Unlike Hebrew, English was not necessarily derived with the clever intention of assigning numeric values to the lettering. However, where English words are derived from ancient roots, gematria may be successful in revealing correlated meanings. There are two words that may be used in the Hebrew translation of "ark". One is *tebah* and means coffin or box. The other is *kaphar.* Kaphar means "to cover over" like the lid on a box or like a "capstone". It also means to atone, which in Mormon theology would mean to make up the difference where man falls short. Mercy fulfills the demands of justice. In Genesis, the Hebrew word kaphar was translated into the English word "pitch" which was used to "seal" the joints of the ark. Kaphar is spelled with a letter kaph, peh and resh from right to left כפר. In English kaph is the letter K and resh is the letter R. The operative consonant sounds in the word ark are the consonants R and K. This is really the key to why an English gematria is productive on the word ark or arc. The English letter R does in fact come from the same ancient glyphs that Hebrew, Egyptian and Canaanite originate from. The English letter R descends from Latin which received it from Greek which received it from Phoenician, which received it from Hebrew. So, the letter R in English and Hebrew share the gematric value of 200. The ancient Hebrew letter R is depicted as the head of a man and means head, chief or top.[2] The letter K descends through the same etymological lineage as R from Hebrew and has the gematric value of 20. This notably is $1/10^{th}$ of the value of K, in the same manner that each of 10 commandments are $1/10^{th}$ of the whole law that was carried in the ark. K descends from the ancient glyph that is depicted as a palm of the hand and means to bend or allow, which carries the geometric connotations of mercy or forgiveness. "Bend" is likely a valid operative meaning when used in "ark". It all roughly seems to convey there is a bending that allows the head of the man to be covered, or that through atonement, the head of the man is sealed. Kaphar is translated often as "mercy seat." The palm of the hand laid upon the head seals a blessing upon the

---

[2] Benner, Jeff A., Ancient Hebrew Research Center.

recipient. A cap is a hat, and it is the root word for captain, who is the head of a boat. A cap is worn on the head. There indeed are valid relationships between these words. Using gematria is one way to open up an exploration in gaining deeper understanding of the intended meanings of words.

There are many other devices that can be used on words after their numeric equivalents are determined. For instance, when the digits 666 are added 6+6+6, the result is the number 18. When the digits are again added the result is the number 9. When the digits of 144,000 are summed 1+4+4+0+0+0 the result is also 9. Thusly, the message conveyed is that the beast and the man that is saved are one and the same.[3] The head of a bull and the body of a man as found in the labyrinth is a symbol for fallen man in a beastly state. It is by subduing the flesh to the will of the Father and by bridling our passions that we gain power to rise and follow the Son of God. The 6 thrice repeated juxtaposed by the 9 denote a transformational process of spiritual growth and gaining further light and knowledge.

---

[3] Hall, Manly P., "The Secret Teachings of All Ages", 1928.

A River Called Sacred Geometry

"Science without religion is lame, religion without science is blind."

–Albert Einstein

Some see that, by definition, true science and true religion can never truly be at odds. And I obviously make that statement true by appending the word "true" to both science and religion. For many thinkers, it has never been considered that spirituality and science were ever unrelated. Isaac Newton, Rennes Descartes, Nicholas Copernicus and many others all spent as much time studying the bible as they did studying their field of mathematics or science. Nevertheless, I wouldn't have to search far to find the doctrines of a false religious belief and couple it with the results of scientific research and find a handful of contradictions. Likewise, there is esoteric knowledge that the spiritually minded of many diverse and even unrelated spiritual traditions have put to the test and find concurrence beyond doubt, yet the scientific forefront still has no detection or measurement method to verify the same experience. However, we can say that if the models or doctrines of either contradict, one of the two needs further improvement or there exists yet a third higher fact to be discovered that reconciles the lesser two. J. Reuben Clark who was an apostle in the Church of Jesus Christ of Latter-day Saints said, "If we have the truth, it cannot be harmed by investigation. If we have not the truth, it ought to be harmed." Men like this in the church embolden my own preference for rigor.

The fact is that neither the body of people associated with the pursuit of science nor the members of the many religions have a perfect knowledge of all things, but each individual in either group do each have a perfect knowledge of some things and they both commonly seek further truth and knowledge. My favorite definition of truth comes from one of the recorded revelations of Joseph Smith, "Truth is the knowledge of things as they are, and as they were, and as they are to come." Furthermore I deduce from several comments made by the statesman, inventor and member of the Rosicrucian Order, Benjamin Franklin, that the two pursuits, scientific and spiritual, may be distinguished by their methods of attaining truth and gaining further enlightenment and knowledge. As Benjamin said, "The way to see by Faith, is to shut the Eye of Reason." When distilled down, these two seemingly contrary methods of learning, in the extreme, are in fact the two pillars of Pythagorean thought....the rational and logical versus the irrational and intuitive. One of the earliest and most ancient and even sacred tools of science and spiritual thinking is geometry. Let's take a look at how geometry has played a key role in the history of spiritual practice, how geometry becomes a medium for sacred thought and what the experiment of faith is.

Geometry since the Beginning

Anciently, the Egyptians that lived on the Nile had an intimate relationship with the living world around them and a vivid awareness of the chaotic forces around them as well. Each year the Nile would flood to cover the farmland along the river and then recede. Because of the alluvial nature of the Nile, the land would look quite different after the chaos of flooding; the farmers would need to re-measure their plots. And because the stars above were in motion they were aware that all around them was in motion. So after the flooding would recede, they would do the work of measuring the land and laying down squares so that it would become ordered again for yet another season. The word "geometry" literally means the "measure of the Earth".[1]

The European Quadrivium was the canon of sciences that pertained to mankind's spatial and temporal existence and their harmony with all that was around them. The quadrivium consisted of four parts: geometry, arithmetic, astronomy and music. Geometry is typically applied to the spatial ordering of matter in the physical plane. If we look at what happens when the Egyptians defined their new plots of farm land using boundaries created by geometry, we can quickly realize that this process is one of the very earliest technologies to facilitate real estate agreements. A defined method of defining geological areas likely prevented contentions and chaos that would otherwise ensue from having unfair land boundary definition. So, geometry is recognized very early on as a way to help establish order and peace in lieu of chaos and contention. This is expressed well in the Masonic principle, "ordo ab chao" which is Latin for "order from chaos". We can see in modern times that similar methods of land surveying have been used as in ancient times. Upon arriving in the Salt Lake Valley, Brigham Young thrust his cane into the soils of the western frontier and declared that they

---

[1] Lawlor, Robert, "Sacred Geometry: Philosophy & Practice", 1982, Thames & Hudson, p 6.

would build a temple to God in that place. John Taylor noted the exact location and that would become the cornerstone location for the great granite temple. Quite near to it a point was established that would also become the rose-line that defines the coordinates and meridians of the western desert basin. Located at that point is a small unassuming monument; an obelisk that stands only a few feet high. A 100 sq-ft astronomical observation station is positioned on Salt Lake City Temple Square as well. The temple, the astronomical observation station and the origin point under the obelisk are three critical tools used to define man's place in the cosmos. Many of the great prophets received specific blue prints directly from God that contained temple dimensions, ark dimensions, City of Jerusalem dimensions. In many families of people we find the application of geometry in their inspired architecture. The temple at Denderah is similar in construction to the temple of Solomon. The pyramids of Egypt use exacting measurements and are a meeting point between the earth and the heavens. There are temples or sacred sites that rely on circular geometry such as the Oracle at Delphi or the stone circles throughout England such as Stonehenge and the great stone circle at Avebury. The Pueblo Bonita kivas at Chaco Canyon in New Mexico are aligned to the four cardinal directions and, like most ancient temples, connect the heavens and earth. They provide a reference point and an advanced measurement system for gauging the movement of the celestial bodies. In the druid cultures of far western Europe, the land itself was believed to have energies that were associated with location on the land.[2] Lines were drawn to span the hills and valleys; they were called ley lines.

---

[2] Queally, Jackie, "The Spiritual Meaning of Rosslyn's Carvings", p.21.

We find that geometric patterns have been prescribed by God to men from ancient times until the present. Preceding the great discoveries in physics were great discoveries in geometry. Isaac Newton is known for producing one of the most thorough artistic drafts of Solomon's temple to this date. The floor plans and architecture of many gothic cathedrals are designed geometrically in the same proportions as the ratios of musical consonance. Solomon's temple itself is designed such that the outer courts are built in ratio of the fourth, the fifth and the octave. The Holy of Holies is based on the 1:1 ratio which is unison and the most perfect of consonances.[3] Because of the harmony in ratio that went in to temple design, much harmony can issue from the temple. Scientific experiment, geometric symbolism and geometric beauty are important parts of understanding religion as we have it today and those parts of our understanding grew out of and can continue to grow out of temple principles.

An arc angle may be expressed trigonometrically by a ratio. The arch angel is known for blowing a trumpet and creating a musical note. Thusly the etymological play on words between the arc angle and arch angel ties together the concept of the geometric ratio and the beauty of music. It is the case too that the geometries of the arches in the cathedral are designed with musical consonance in their ratio.

What is amazing is that we can find that geometric symbols may be assigned with ease to an ancient lesson in the Book of Mormon that fuses the scientific method with the spiritual experiment, revealing the path to enlightenment. The process is documented in the Book of Alma in a beautiful allegory. In

---

[3] Strachnan, Gordon, "Chartres: Sacred Geometry, Sacred Space", p.46,47

Alma chapter 32 the "hypothesis" is likened to a seed. The seed is referred to as the seed of faith. After all, a hypothesis is an unproven postulate and is the element of faith. Alma reveals how to turn a spiritual hypothesis into knowledge. Let's examine Alma's lesson and assign geometric symbols. Before proceeding, let's recall that Benjamin Franklin once said that to see with the eye of faith, one must close the eye of reason. Let's consider that in the process of enlightenment, an act of faith precedes the acquisition of the substance upon which reason may build.

Alma and the Experiment of Faith[4]

The practices of the sciences are not only enriching, inspiring and wondrous, but the work done in science helps dispel false notions, superstitions and in some cases diminishes what were anciently termed as false priestcrafts. Science need not stand alone uncoupled with its spiritual counterpart. As an example, we may consider that Elijah had harnessed the power of the priesthood of God when he displayed great scientific wonders in harmony with divine physical and spiritual powers and principles. Through this act he dispelled the false priestcrafts amongst the people of Ahab. The ancient American prophet and seer named Alma had personal experience in leaving a false priestcraft and afterwards he experience a change of heart. Alma records lessons that he gleaned from his experience and the revelations that he'd received. He provides a wonderful procedure with which to perform the "experiment of faith". Let's follow through his thinking, while using geometric symbols

---

[4] Alma 32: 27-43

to represent the principles that Alma teaches in metaphor. This could not be done with such continuity with just any lesson on faith, but Alma's reasoning and select choice of metaphoric symbols follow eternal creation principles and correct universal archetypes. Furthermore, the words Joseph Smith was inspired to use in his work lend to an exacting congruence between principle and symbol.

"Behold if ye will awake and arouse your faculties, even to an experiment upon my words, and exercise a particle of faith, yea, even if ye can no more than desire to believe, let this desire work in you, even until ye believe in a manner that ye can give place for a portion of my words." (Alma 32:27)

Alma requests that we prepare by providing enough room for a "portion" of his words. Since this means roughly several of his words, let's make sure our paper is large enough to contain them.

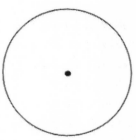

XXXI. Spiritual seed

"Now, we will compare the word to a seed." (Alma 32:28)

First, plant a seed in our heart, or in the earth. Let's start by drawing a point because a seed is small like a point. It is a spiritual seed. It is yet in its form as one. (Alma 32:28)

We can let the seed swell like a ripple in still water after a pebble is dropped into it. The way we will geometrically represent this is by placing the point of the compass to the origin and by circumscribing a complete circle around the origin point. The span of the compass sets the bounds of the Lord. We also discussed while in the Cathedral that the circle represents the

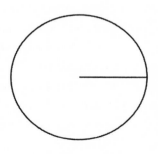

XXXII. Radius and Circle

womb or gestation fields; the soil that is aerated by the plough pulled by the ox. In this case, Alma establishes that the planting field for the seed is our heart. Let this circle also represent the presence of God and the celestial and spiritual aspect of the Garden of Eden before the fall; infinite, unified, whole. Mark a second point on the circumference of the circle that is roughly horizontal from the origin point. If the circle were a navigational compass with cardinal directions, place the point in the East direction for the tree of life was planted eastward in the Garden of Eden and draw a line segment to this point.

Keeping the same radius on the compass, use this point on the circle of the first as the center around which to draw a second circle. Now we see the duality that emerges. If the second circle were a navigational compass, the line segment would be pointing West; which is the opposite of East. The second

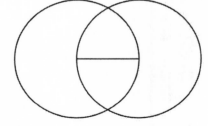

XXXIII. The circle to the left represents the spiritual feminine and the circle to the right represents the temporal feminine; the radius represents the Word of God

circle presents duality as do the two horns of the ox or apis, however, accompanying duality is balance. The line segment thusly represents duality and also balance. Since Adam and Eve partook of the fruit, they fell and the earth ceased to remain in the presence of God. Let the second circle represent earth in its present state; finite, disjointed; broken yet contrite. The second circle is a reflection of the first, just as our earthly home is a reflection of our heavenly home. In the extreme, the natural man is an enemy to God and the fallen nature of earth is in direct opposition to the celestial order of our first home in the pre-existence.

We recall that in the beginning God allowed there to be light. The simplest and most natural representation for the origin of light is a "point source". This is always represented diagrammatically by a point. Because modern physics has discerned that light operates both as a particle and a wave, both the line segment and the circle represent the propagation of light. This duality of the nature of light at first is a challenge to understand and was modeled by the DeBroglie equation $hv=mc^2$. Until the physics student performs the necessary optical experiments, the equation is used on faith because of the simple fact that what it claims is not logical to our objective mind. Electromagnetic waves of light propagate radially from the light point source in the same way waves propagate like ripples in water away from a pebble with some wave frequency, without mass, yet as pure energy. However, when light also behaves like a particle it moves in a straight line with velocity and mass. This duality is something that we work with in light physics.

Just as God said "let there be light", in Alma's operation Alma instructs us to do no more than give the seed a place in our heart and to not cast it out by unbelief. Belief allows the warmth of the Spirit of the Lord to speak with light to the seed. Thusly the line segment between the point in the heavenly circle represents a fluence of light from the presence of God to the earthly circle. Thusly, while on earth in its fallen state we are promised that if we keep his commandments to be "like him" or a reflection of Christ, we are promised that we may have the Spirit of the Lord and that we may be at-one with him. Thusly, the area of the intersecting circles with line segment connecting the "centers" represents "atonement". We may also duly use the word "atunement", like when tuning a musical instrument. When light propagates radially from the point source, the wave form has a frequency just in the same manner that a musical note has a frequency. A musical experiment demonstrates the analog of this principle. If we place two tuning forks of the same size, shape and note next to each other but with some small distance between them, we can then strike one tuning fork to create a vibration. This vibration will cause the second tuning fork to begin to hum in the same frequency and note. So, by shaping and sizing our life after the pattern set by the Lord, by lifting up our eyes and looking upon the fields, always striving to have the image of the Savior in our countenance we may find ourselves in harmony with him and find energy to perform the Great and Marvelous Work.

Arc angles are representative of motion and the power to move; motion is inherently implied by the geometric circle. "When you begin to feel these swelling 'motions', ye will begin to say within yourselves-It must needs be that this is a good seed." (Alma 32:28) The two separate circles, in a sense, also represent the breasts from which nourishment is received by the infant from the mother, as well as where these swelling motions are felt. In some other applications, these two circles represent the sun and the moon and, therefore, it is allowable to assign the symbols of the square and compass as well.

"It must needs be that this is a good seed, or that the word is good." The word of the Lord, as represented by the line segment drawn between the two circles, is thusly deductively concluded by Alma to have been present and "good" due to the feeling of swelling in the breasts. So, in Alma's experimental methodology, it is the swelling in the breasts, the enlargement of the soul, the enlightenment of understanding and the deliciousness of the experience that are the measurable results of the experiment of faith. In the scientific method, it is the measurable and repeatable results that indicate, whether directly or indirectly, to our objective senses that we may conclude that a hypothesis is good. Notice that Alma does not ask the student yet if this experience is "real" because we are still working in the realm of faith; Ben Franklin's eye of reason is yet closed. He only asks if it "feels" good. He is not calling upon objective senses in his experimental metrology. In a sense, drawing the line segment across the radius of the circle represents walking by faith or the attributes of faith. Alma asks his student, "Now behold would not this increase your faith?" He confirms the correct answer that naturally arises from within, "I say unto you, Yea." He then goes on to qualify this by saying, "Nevertheless it hath not grown up to a perfect knowledge". There is more to do. There is more geometry to represent what is done as well.

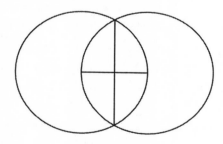

XXXIV. The word sprouteth; the sprout is both metaphorically and geometrically the "square root " of three.

There are many viable next steps we could take in our geometric drawing, however, Alma the teacher mentions that the seed "swelleth, and sprouteth, and beginneth to grow" three times. The emphasis here is on three times. He gets the attention of the student, saying, "But behold, as the seed swelleth, and sprouteth, and beginneth to grow, then you must needs say that the seed is good; for behold it swelleth, and sprouteth, and beginneth to grow. And now, behold, will not this strengthen your faith? Yea, it will strengthen your faith: for ye will say I know that this is a good seed; for behold it sprouteth and beginneth to grow." Looking for an obvious sprouting forth from the seed, we draw the following lines, "sprouting", as it were, from the line segment. I can't help but recall the Jesse Window with the sprouting posterity growing forth vertically from the seed of his loins. The sprouting line is vertically drawn between the intersections of the circles. Just as earth, sun and the nourishment of seasonal water combine with the seed to sprout a plant, the circles and line segment are combined to yield our geometric representation of the sprouting. In the Jesse Window, the vertical line, or stem, sprouting up caused us to consider it as a symbol of strength as it looked much like a vertically ascending spine with Jesse himself as the root. The spine is the source of strength. Alma asks the question, "And now, will not this strengthen your faith?"

The pleasant thing about geometry is that reliance on intuition is met mercifully in this practice. Whenever the compass scribes out a circle, we may know its radius is 1 and therefore any point along the circumference is also 1 from the origin of that circle. Holding on to this allows for fairly simple geometric logic to be applied to geometric shapes that result. We observed the symbolism expand from a seed that is represented by a point and represents unity into a representation of duality and thusly moving that seed from a heavenly presence to a temporal presence and furthermore giving it the duality of the heavenly and the earthly. We discovered the third quality of atonement. Atonement is associated with the number symbol 3. The number 3 is represented by the triangle. Using a straight edge, let's connect the geometric points that rise intuitively.

Two triangles are thusly drawn. The triangle represents *perfect manifestation*. These triangles are equilateral, meaning each side is the same length as the other. The proof may be followed through by examining that the distance from origin to circumference is unity or 1 for each circle and each of the sides of the triangle is in itself the radius of either one circle or the other. This figure is also another archetypal symbol of the seed. It is in the likeness of the parent seed that preceded this child seed. All that we see now in our

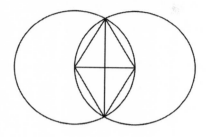

XXXV. Alma relates "three" times that the word sprouteth; this may be represented by the two triangles. The seed becomes representative of three dimensional expansion of space. The geometric figure within the vesica piscis appears as the side of an octahedron.

drawing was inherently encoded within the heavenly and infinite spiritual DNA of the seed. This is the seed that has expanded somewhat, but according to Alma is not yet "real"; it is not yet objective knowledge. The triangle is a perfect representation of a 2 dimensional plane. We have considered the East and West directions, which are two directions or one axis. When we added the strength of the spine, or the vertical line segment, we added another axis which was truly a component of the circles we scribed. The triangle above and the triangle below, defined by the cross inside, also remind us of our discussion on the crucifixion of Jesus the Christ on the cross; there were three men, each hung on a cross in the air above, and three women standing on the earth below. The triangle above may symbolize the male attributes and the triangle below may symbolize the female attributes. In Chartres, the male attributes are emphasized in the Jesse Window above and collecting the light or fire element of the sun as do branches and leaves of a tree. The labyrinth emphasizes the feminine attributes and is below bearing the waters of nourishment and womb as do the earth and tree roots. If we look at the two triangles we may see how they, together as a plane, form the base of a tetrahedron or a four sided pyramid as viewed in a skewed manner. They also form the side view of two pyramids base-to-base; the one pointing up and the other down. Thusly, the pyramid holds symbolic meaning akin to a tree.

Again, Alma's message is that "every seed bringeth forth its likeness". In the context of a tree the seed that is brought forth doesn't occur until fruit is born and picked. However, following Alma's procedure, we are not that far, yet we may expect that we will find likeness in many ways long before we find real fruit.

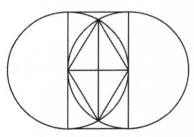

XXXVI. The square represents the earth in its four quarters and also Adam; the squares as drawn also depict "The Stem of Jesse" that holds the seed that begets Jesus.

Let's draw, in the likeness of the seed; that which represents the word, both line segments above and below.

Take the straight edge and trace a line from the tangents of the two circles. This now creates two squares; one above and one below. Very good! This brings us up through verse 33. Alma the teacher then asks the student,

"Behold is your knowledge perfect?" Alma then confirms the answers that the sincere student would then have searched out and surely have discovered for himself or herself in his or her heart and mind, "Yeah your knowledge is perfect in that thing, and your faith is dormant; and this is because you know that the word hath swelled your souls, and ye also know that it hath sprouted up, that your understanding doth begin to be enlightened, and your mind doth begin to expand. O then is not this real? I say unto you, Yea, because it is light and whatsoever is light, is good because it is discernible."

So, in completing the square, we have moved from the realm of faith in the unseen to the realm of the objectively enlightening! Ben Franklin may now close the eye of faith as the eye of reason opens. When the branches and roots of the triangle are discerned and the square is drawn, we are objectively seeing in greater light the symbolism of the tree; the actual elements that feed and nourish the tree. The four sides of the square suggest objective "reality" as found in the basic symbols which the swelling of the seed brought forth: air, earth, water and fire. It is in the cube also that three dimensions are manifested and this is where life happens! That which is spiritual is now fully clothed in the material of life and takes its seat in the physical realm.[5] In fact, if we look at the image, we see that adding those final lines completed the tail section of what looks like a fish! This was in fact the manner of derivation of the ancient symbol of Jesus Christ and also a symbol of the age of Pisces. This is how this symbol came to be called the vesica piscis. To successfully have followed this lesson of Alma truly brings us to a celebratory resting point here as Alma concludes that our

---

[5] Refers back to "Isaac Newton and the Throne of Gravity" on p. 125.

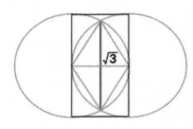

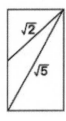

XXXVII. 1, √2, √3 and √5 are roots of the metaphoric tree and are the mathematical square "roots".

knowledge is perfect in this thing. With the completion of the square, we gain a second witness that within this geometric method we have all the tools needed to continue to derive the Platonic polygons.

Now, we may notice that in order to draw the lines tangent to the circles, we had to draw "outside" of the circles. If the circles represent the two aspects of being in the garden, first the spiritual and secondly the physical, drawing the line segment outside of the circles which completes the square creates a symbolic situation where the square, representing Adam, begins to move out of the garden, first spiritually then physically; yet his origins and attributes will remain ever "rooted" in the garden that is his origin. Alma asks, "after ye have *tasted* this light is your knowledge perfect?" Alma's reference to "tasting light" poetically emphasizes that the light of knowledge is synonymous with the fruit of the tree of knowledge. We may then ask ourselves in the spirit of Benjamin Franklin, now that our eye of reason opens, need we close the eye of faith ever more? No, heavens no! Our work is not done. As the teacher, Alma, instructs "Behold I say unto you, Nay, neither must ye lay aside your faith for ye have only exercised your faith to plant the seed that ye might try the experiment to know if the seed was good. And behold as the tree beginneth to grow, ye will say, "Let us nourish it with great care."

Alma then instructs us on the next steps of the operation. "And behold, as the tree beginneth to grow, ye will say: Let us nourish it with great care that it may get *root*, and grow up, and bring forth fruit." So, this instruction suggests that the tree will continue to get root if we do this step with care. The roots are found in the diagonals of the geometric squares. The root gives foundation to the tree. The roots extract water and nutrients from the earth to sustain the boughs and fruits of the tree. The squares are representative of the earth and also of our heart when contrite with eternal laws. Alma's words then give instruction to the student about the next steps of the operation with admonitions to be diligent and patient, warning that "if ye will not nourish the word, looking forward *with an eye of faith* to the fruit thereof, ye can never pluck of the fruit of the tree of life". (Hey, there's Ben's eye of faith!) Did we know when we began this experiment that what we nourished would grow into a tree of life symbol? Alma, then assures the students as if they were present, "Then my brethren, ye shall reap the rewards of your faith, and your diligence and patience and long-suffering, waiting for the tree to bring forth fruit unto you"; a fruit that is "most precious, which is sweet above all that is sweet, and which is white above all that is white, yea and pure above all that is pure." We discover that this tree has white fruit that is pure above all that is pure and sweet above all that is sweet. It becomes clear that Alma knew of and had personally applied principles common with the vision that Lehi had; the vision of the Tree of Life. Furthermore, Alma's approach to teaching the experiment of faith couples with great fidelity to the universal archetypes of illumination extracted from geometric symbolism.

Part IV
The Lehi Key

XXXVIII. Lehi partakes of the fruit of the Tree of Life. Watercolor by Annie Aronson.

Branches of an Egyptian Tree

In the days of Lehi predating 600 B.C., astronomy, geometry and mathematics were taught in the Egyptian mystery schools. Pythagoras of Samos was born in about 570 B.C., only 30 years after Lehi's migration away from the Mediterranean.

Similar to Lehi, Pythagoras left the Eastern Mediterranean and started his philosophical order in the midst of a pre-existing culture. He went to Italy. He had previously been initiated into the mysteries of Byblos and Tyre and discovered that they taught after the manner of the Egyptian mysteries which piqued his interest to go to Egypt. He spent, some say, 22 years in Egypt studying in the temples where he learned about geometry and astronomy. Unlike Lehi, who was inspired to leave and go into the wilderness, Pythagoras received no impressions that he should leave and was consequently taken captive by the Babylonians. While in captivity he managed to profit from the experience and further learned Babylonian mathematics from the magi and after 12 years left to return to Samos. Meanwhile, across the waters, Lehi's family had successfully established themselves in what is now called the American continent. There were several groups that left from the area fleeing Babylonian rule. After his return from Babylon, Pythagoras journeyed to Italy to live amongst the thinkers of the day. While the branch of Lehi's family called the Nephites had established a temple after the manner of Solomon, Pythagoras started an order and culture in Italy known as the Cenobites. They were in number about 2000 which included their wives and their children. Both Lehi and Pythagoras herald from the Egyptian tradition. Whether it's through the tradition of Moses established in the House of Israel or learned directly from his own initiation into the Egyptian mysteries, one way or the other Egyptian thinking is found in Lehi's teachings to his sons. Lehi's family's preference for writing was to use modified Egyptian characters.

In the mystery school of Pythagoras, the initiates would spend the first five years only allowed to listen and not allowed to speak directly face to face with Pythagoras. The initiates were referred to as the *akousmatekoi* and would be taught by Pythagoras who would instruct them from behind a veil. After 5 years, those who met his criteria for entrance would be elevated to the level of *esoterics,* who were then permitted to enter beyond the veil and be instructed personally face to face by Pythagoras. Esoterics were considered to be the living and any who were rejected from the school were considered to be dead. A modern Mormon colloquial equivalent might be "active" versus "inactive".

There have been many different initiatory mystery groups throughout time. The mysteries of Eleusis were noted by Cicero who stated, "For it appears to me that among the many exceptional and divine things your Athens has produced and contributed to human life, nothing is better than those mysteries. For by means of them we have transformed from a rough and savage way of life to the state of humanity, and have been civilized. Just as they are called initiations, so in actual fact we have learned from them the fundamentals of life, and have grasped the basis not only for living with joy but also for dying with a better hope."[1]

The mysteries have always been taught in various forms of temples and the temple traditions and rituals vary in content, but with the general purpose of raising a group of people to a more ordered and enlightened manner of living. Little is ever known of what goes on inside as each group typically makes a covenant to keep what is learned and experienced inside sacred. Most scholarly treatises on the Eleusinian ceremony acknowledge immediately that so little is known about what they actually did

---

[1] Cicero, Marcus Tullius, *De Legibus*.

that beyond some few simple understandings most discussion is conjecture.

The general sequence of a ceremony consists of some sort of initiation which is presented in a drama as conflict, a wound or entry into a world of chaos and darkness. Some sort of messenger from the woods, the heavens or the king visits the initiate and elevates them with esoteric knowledge. There are typically tests and passing through veils. The 7 veils of Isis are also represented as 7 scorpions. The mists of Avalon presumably serve as a veil. Christian Rosenkreutz passes through three gates and then must be weighed on a scale. The veil does two opposite things. The challenge to the seeker is that it obscures the path or presents trials. However, the veil also plays an important function and protects the sanctity of the core (Kore) within, and also the seed of the Tree of Life. Many of the profane are turned away from progressing, often never knowing they have left the course. Even the elect of God may be led astray. While this may be considered a tragedy in some regards, in other regards it is prudence that they are turned back that they may learn the important lessons needed to be prepared to progress, as other trials will certainly be presented. Line upon line and precept upon precept we progress. As we falter, the merciful hand of the Lord is extended to us. His atonement in our behalf grants us a path of redemption if we will seek it.

Lehi Encounters the Tree of Life

One of the most beautiful and amazing testimonies of divine teaching by God grows from the observation that the Tree of Life shows up in so many times, cultures and places and the same eternal truths are revealed. Now, in some traditions God the Father may be referred to as Cosmic Consciousness, Elohim, being both male and female gods, or the Divine. I am so happy that anyone strives to establish conscious contact with our higher power that I have no concern by what names someone knows God or the Gods. Whatever it is they call God, when they describe his attributes, I know we are talking about the same all powerful, all kind and loving, just and merciful deity. I suspect God is not so concerned about what you call him so long as you call him. I like that Masons often call him The Great Architect. If some culture referred to the Sun as the god, I understand what they mean when they acknowledge that warmth that comes from the sun and its life sustaining properties, for yet they recognize a higher power than themselves.

We are born of Heavenly parents, both a Heavenly Mother and a Heavenly Father. In Mormon tradition, holy sacredness is given to Heavenly Mother and very little is verbally said about her, with the purpose that the profane never *see* or understand her quintessential role so that sacred learnings may be kept as a flame within rather than without. Yet, it is well known and both exoterically and esoterically understood that family is the most important part of the Plan of Our Father in Heaven. The man and woman as husband and wife and father and mother are central to the esoteric teachings of cosmic balance and harmony.

One of the great stories in the Book of Mormon is of a mystic vision that Lehi has. It is known as "Lehi's Dream", though I would suggest he was not asleep, but rather he was in meditation. In his dream he sees a dark and dreary wilderness akin to what is known in some alchemical traditions as the dark night of the soul. The dark night of the soul is a requisite cycle in life that occurs typically for the sages throughout time in their mid-thirties. Buddha became Buddha at age 35 and Jesus Christ died on the cross at age 34. Robert Bly points out in his contemplation of the Grimm fairy tale, Iron John, that in stage progression a man grows through three fundamental phases. He refers to them as the red knight, the white knight and the black knight phases. The red knight phase happens in our youth and it is typified by positive youthful energy, a general recklessness and a lack of wisdom. Using a fishing metaphor, the fisherman in the red knight phase catches lots of small yet easy-to-catch fish. In the context of the Mormon experience, the white knight phase is typically when a young man goes off to serve as a missionary. He is the knight in shining armor, he is the embodiment of good and life seems as if evil is only on the outside of him and is some external enemy to be fought. The black knight phase is less understood it seems. This is the man that discovers the evils within and begins to recognize the old wounds from whence they issue. He runs into himself and his own seemingly irreconcilable conflict. He stops seeing evil as an external force alone that has waged war on him from without and considers that many of his evils come from within. The wounds incurred in his younger years catch up with him and he must look squarely in the eye at the nature of death if he is to progress. He learns to sit with his wounds and accept his feelings when the cycle of putrefaction of his soul sets in. This is where men fail to become men all too often in our day and age. This is where the midlife crisis plays out and seeks to maintain youthfulness at the cost of spirituality and conscious communion with God, who rules in the heavens above and in the earth beneath. (Abraham 3:21). For the religious disciple, this is where the old bottle fails to hold new wine and old things must become as new. Bly discusses the idea of going through the ashes of our burnt up life one spoonful at a time to look at things carefully.[2] This ascension and rising from the ashes might be likened unto Icarus stitching his feathers back together that he may ascend from the waters of death and learn to fly while avoiding extremes; and thusly wear the crown of gold even as Horus is depicted in the Book of Abraham.

I believe this developmental phase is all akin to the dark and dreary wilderness that Lehi must walk through. Yet, as in spiritual recovery and personal healing, while it is an inner spiritual work, one need not go through this process alone. In the dream of Lehi a man dressed in a white robe comes and stands next to him. It is never explained who the man in the white robe is. It may be an angel, it may be the Lord, and it may, in fact, be Lehi himself. Dream symbols are often parts of our own self. Lehi while in the dark and dreary waste seems to feel stuck and calls upon the Lord to have mercy on him. Mercy claimeth her own and so with that measure that Lehi had rendered mercy unto others in his days, so too was it returned unto him and he passed through his dark night of the soul at last to go forth beyond the darkness and partake of the fruit of the Tree of Life.

---

[2] Robert Bly, "Iron John: A Book About Men", 2004, De Capo Press.

Dreams take place predominantly in the subconscious realm, and so objective information flow is small during the dream state. Some amount of intermittent subjective thought takes place. During sleep our subconscious minds are assimilating information, attempting to chunk and order together all of the information taken in to our minds through the course of living; both information we are aware of but also a much, much greater portion of information that we didn't consciously notice. Some of that information becomes valuable in the dream. Calling upon the Lord for mercy is successful contingent upon our willingness to let go of things that we don't truthfully have power or influence over. At one point in my life while learning to fall asleep in times of stress, I imagined my grandmother who had passed on being on the other side of the veil, knitting dreams for me as I sleep. The more I let go of trying to manage my own mental faculties, the more mental yarn is yielded up to my grandmother beyond the veil to mend my wounds and heal my soul. Whether that was creative imagery of my own or a veiled allegory of how things really work, this is, in part, one way that mercy may claim *her* own.

As Lehi is recovered from the dark and dreary wilderness, he then sees a great and spacious field and in the midst of it is a tree. As we read about the Lehi's tree of life, we may ask ourselves whether it is like the Tree of Life that was in the Garden in Eden. Yes, it is. The transition through the dark and dreary wilderness to arrive at the field and tree is, in fact, a passing beyond a type of veil for Lehi. If we do think of all of the parts of Lehi's dream to be parts of Lehi himself, then we may consider that we find another attribute of the dark knight phase to be the discovery of the creative space within. The spacious field is the creative ground upon which creative endeavors may transpire. We find a garden inside of us; it is ours to create. It is the place within our mind where we build a spiritual temple. Its dressing and upkeep require spiritual upkeep.

Lehi's journey to the Tree of Life is a fatherly journey for he arrives at the tree and beholds the fruit of the tree that it is white; it makes him happy and he wants the rest of his family to partake of it. In his meditation, it is not by the dream symbol of the iron rod that Lehi arrives at the tree; yet it is by the word of God just the same. However, it is by the symbol of the iron rod that his sons and wife will make their journey if they choose to.

The Tree of Life shows up in many traditions and each seems to tell the same story in different ways. Some traditions offer an entirely interactive experience where one is immersed in an ascension drama or temple ritual. The Tree of Life that Lehi beheld is also represented by the Qabalah in the Hebrew and Egyptian influenced hermetic tradition. It is represented by the Tetractys in the Pythagorean teachings. It is represented by Egyptian hieroglyphs in the Book of Abraham. Joseph Smith Jr. sees the highest level of abstraction or the macrocosmic level of the Tree of Life in the Book of Abraham Facsimile 2 and he describes the principles as they relate to creation and the keys of the priesthood. In the case of Facsimile 2, the balance of male and female participation in the priesthood governance of creation is expressed.

The Qabalah, Tetractys and Abraham Facsimile 2 all describe the thing. Let's consider some of the commonalities by contemplating the key symbols in each rendition of the Tree of Life first. Before continuing I should state a few assumptions that I am building on. Firstly, I am keeping open to Hugh Nibley's conjecture that Osiris and Abraham may be considered to have been the same man and thusly that Isis and Sariah may be considered to be the same woman. If not literally the same, then at least their characteristics are commonly typal enough to be represented by shared symbols. Abram, later called Abraham, had a history of name changes; it's not unheard of. Additionally, whether the hypocephalus in the Pearl of Great Price was written by Abraham or *the hand* of Abraham, where the hand of Abraham might be a traditional adherent named Sheshonq, or whether the model of the hypocephalus was literally written by Abraham, it doesn't matter to me. I will interchangeably refer to Abraham Facsimile 2 as the hypocephalus or at times as the Sheshonq hypocephalus.

The Book of Abraham and Qabalah

Joseph Smith assigned names to Egyptian hieroglyphs and hieratics that are different than the names assigned by modern professionals in the fields of archaeology and Egyptology. For instance, in the hypocephalus also known as Facsimile 2, Joseph assigns the name Olibish to the character that is commonly referred to as Ra or Horus and then refers to that character as God. Abraham is the name Joseph uses to represent Osiris. What is this mystery? Knowledge of Osiris was clearly available in the 1840's in New England and the frontier as demonstrated by the presence of the Rosicrucians and the descriptive details on Osiris in Morals and Dogma by Albert Pike. The era from 1808 to 1858 has been known as the Egyptian Revival Era[3] and I believe that Joseph was neither naive nor ignorant of the rising

---

[3] Carrot, Richard G., "Egyptian Revival: Its Sources, Monuments and Meanings, 1808–1858", printed in 1978.

Egyptian movement of his day. Joseph also knew that his ability to interpret the hypocephalus was in fact limited. He makes this clear when he admits that certain characters in the hypocephalus

XXXIX. Abraham Facsimile 2 from the Times and Seasons, 1842.

are just simply not being revealed to him by the Lord, whereas some characters are. In the Facsimile 2 interpretation, we find the absolutely most mysterious, cosmic and mystical principles taken right from an Egyptian hypocephalus and written in terms of priesthood keys, names and authority but also in terms of light, light mediums, time and other essential and fundamental principles of physics. The close relationship between physical principles and spiritual principles is a key distinguishing characteristic of Joseph's interpretation.

Abraham himself is a type of an omega relative to the Egyptian kingdom and an alpha relative to the birth of the Abrahamic family from which Judaism eventually grows out of. Growing out of Judaism we find teachings and traditions that can be compared with the Egyptian traditions. Let's first take a look at similarities between Joseph's interpretation of the Egyptian hypocephalus and the Hebrew based hermetic Qabalah that developed with an influx from Hebrew tradition starting as early as the 1300's in Europe.

It is known that in ancient temple dramas, one person will play a role that represents either another person or a body of attributes, virtues or principles. What becomes important isn't the specificity of names, but rather the principles or functions that the roles represent. We strive to become like Jesus and we may even take his name upon us. We are admonished by Isaiah to be saviors on Mount Zion. We benefit spiritually from striving to rise up and walk in the footsteps of the Lord and by so doing we also bless the lives of others around us by emulating his attributes.

Earlier in this book we looked at the utility of using numeric equivalencies to analyze the meanings of words. Specifically, gematria was co-developed with Hebrew lettering, however, we also know that hermetic Qabalists have used gematria in English, French and Latin. While it serves to explore or establish the connectedness of ideas, their unity and relatedness, gematria is used in the European hermetic tradition to convey messages. For instance, it may be used to show equivalency of meaning. Two words with numeric equivalents may be explored for common or related meanings. While some may employ this in a sort of literary recreation with a poetic lawlessness about it, some may only wish to use it as a device for analysis. For the latter use, some amount of validation and verification is then warranted. So, let's take a look at the most prominent name in the Book of Abraham Facsimile 2 and the meaning associated with it.

To the Abraham Facsimile 2, fig. 1 Joseph assigns the name *Kolob*. Let's first look at the gematria. Since there are no vowels in Hebrew, let's remove them, leaving us with KLB. K, Q and C, if pronounced with a hard K sound, may all be assigned either the number 20 or 100. For the sake of this effort, let's start with 20. The next letter L is assigned the number 30. The letter B is assigned the number 2. Adding the values, we arrive at 20+30+2 = 52. Let's now take the word Qabalah and do the same. Removing the vowels we are left with QBL. The values are 20+2+30 = 52. So, by this method of gematria, KLB is equivalent in meaning to KBL and thusly QBL. Therefore, the deeper meanings of Kolob and Qabalah can be hypothesized to be equivalent. This is to say that the hermetic Qabalah and the Egyptian hypocephalus convey information about the same thing. Well, the fact is that gematria can be employed in several ways so that anything could be found to be related to anything. So let's compare the very basic elements of the hermetic Qabalah with the basic elements of the Abraham (Sheshonq) hypocephalus and see what comes out of this experiment.

The Macrocosm

The word macrocosm heralds from the medieval latin *macrocosmus* which means the 'great world'. It is the whole of the universe. Carl Jung refers to the symbol of the Cosmic Man as being the great external Self.[4] In this sense the man in the white robe that visits Lehi in his dream may be the macroscopic Self of Lehi. The man in the white robe is in fact the Tree itself and furthermore is the Self of Lehi in his dream. It is attributed to the teachings of Pythagoras that, "To know thyself is to know the universe and the Gods."

When I studied physics we would always set up the equations for modeling the charge on a conductive sphere by looking at the inside, the outside and the interface. Similarly, our body is the temple of God and when we are talking about the temple, we are also therefore talking about what's going on inside of us, outside of us and at the interface. Therefore, let's look at the inside, the outside and the interface.

Now it's a fact that it is just plain tricky to compare hermetic Qabalah and the Book of Abraham Facsimile 2 Egyptian hypocephalus without running into plenty of discontinuities. Because their geometries are different, the messages conveyed will naturally be distinct also. Nevertheless, it is the case that all that is in motion, in circulation and in revolution in the hypocephalus and Qabalah is also in motion, circulation and revolution in the cosmos around us and reflected within us. There is a flux of light that pulsates through the levels or spheres of creation in the same living way that blood circulates through the veins of our earthly and mortal body. Let's first consider the case of the cosmos that is physically on the outside of us; the heavens above, the earth beneath and the interface. Let's look at the Tree of Life from the outside in, and from the top level down first.

---

[4] Jung, Carl, "Man and his Symbols", 1964, Aldus Books, p. 196-211.

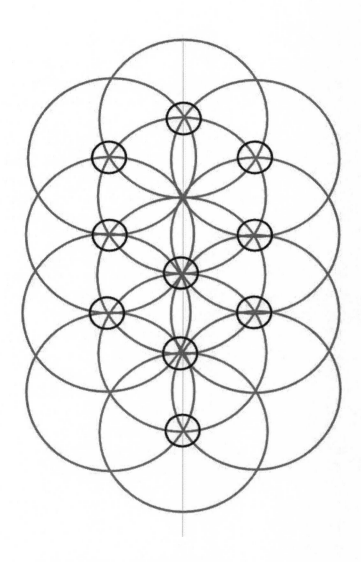

XL.   *The Tree of Life sephiroth can be drawn with a compass.*

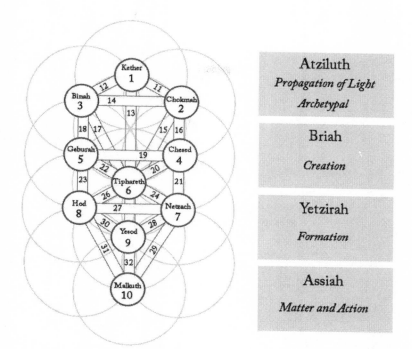

XLI. *The Hermetic Qabalah model of the Tree of Life is made of 10 sephiroth and 22 paths of light flux.*

Sephiroth	Name	Creative Level
1	Kether	Atziluth
2	Chokmah	Atziluth
3	Binah	Atziluth
4	Chesed	Briah
5	Geburah	Briah
6	Tiphareth	Briah
7	Netzach	Yetzirah
8	Hod	Yetzirah
9	Yesod	Yetzirah
10	Malkuth	Assiah

Level 1: Kolob and Atziluth

"Kolob, signifying the first creation, nearest to the celestial, or the residence of God. First in government, the last pertaining to the measurement of time. The measurement according to celestial time signifies one day to a cubit. One day in Kolob is equal to a thousand years according to the measurement of this earth, which is called by the Egyptians Jah-oh-eh."[5] So, within

XLII. Kolob or the Qabalistic world of the archetypal. Here the two gibbons represent Thoth, as well as the principle of the two pillars or Ma'at.

the interpretation is the Alpha-Omega element. It explains how Kolob is both the first and the last and therefore emanates an Alpha and Omega function. It is the first with regards to space and government yet the last with regards to time. It is clarified by Abraham that Kolob was "after the manner of the Lord, according to its times and seasons". It is a *reflection* of the attributes of the Lord. It is also assigned a ratio of 1000 days on

earth to 1 day of celestial time. This may be taken to be strictly physical, but again may be communicating in number symbolism what 1000 represents, which is the omniscience, omnipresence and omnipotence of God. 1000 may also be expressed as 10 x 10 x 10 which, notably, are the dimensions of the Holy of Holies of

---

[5] Smith, Joseph "Abraham Facsimile 2", Interpretation Footnote 1, Pearl of Great Price.

Solomon's temple. Expressing 1000 like this emphasizes that light emanates in the three axes that in Qabalah are represented by the three mother letters: Aleph, Mem and Shin. In Qabalah, the three mother letters represent the first emanations of God that stretch forth to create space itself as well as the first elements of fire, water and air. We also considered earlier how 10 represents "all of a part". So in this sense, Kolob also represents "all of a part". And since Kolob is a reflection of the "manner of the Lord", the figure represents the "all of a part" nature of the Lord; this being his nature due to the work of atonement that he performed. This "all of a part" deity is also typified by the resurrected Osiris. So to summarize, figure 1 does indeed represent emanations of space including an origin. It does contain the number symbol 1000 of omniscience, omnipresence and omnipotence. It is the highest or most celestial level. In Qabalah, this is equivalent to the level of Atziluth which is the archetypal world; the world that projects archetypes such that all else is "after the manner of" Kolob and a reflection of it. This is the highest of four Qabalistic levels. It is the level of Elohim, where female and male deities reside. The Yod or letter Y of the Hebrew Tetragrammaton is associated with this level. This Kolob level is the highest of four orders or four spheres of creation represented by the four beasts in the Book of Revelations as Joseph Smith learns directly from the Lord. The Kolob level is the "last pertaining to the measurement of time". This seems to denote that the time of God is infinite and that due to the infinite nature of the residing place of God, he may be in connection with all things. A reasonable term for this time-independent omniscience is *cosmic consciousness*. However, Kolob is only a level or a place; the "residence of God". When Jesus ascended above all things[6], he likely ascended to this level.

At this point, we may be well convinced that the application of gematria to the words Kolob and Qabalah has uncovered that the numeric equivalents of KLB and QBL also lead us to consider what a comparison of the Egyptian hypocephalus model of the cosmos with the Qabalistic model of the cosmos might yield. So, starting with Kolob, we may expect to find three lower levels or "spheres of creation". The subsequent three levels in the Qabalah below Atziluth would be Briah, Yetzirah and Assiah. Whereas Kolob corresponds directly with Atziluth, the following three levels will correspond directly with the Qabalistic levels: Olibish, Enish-go-on-dosh and the Earth in its four quarters.

Having discussed the archetypes of emanations issuing forth from Kolob or the level of Atziluth to the lower levels, we find the exact same archetypes reflected in the next level below; in the level of Briah.

Level 2: Olibish and Briah

The next sphere of creation is Olibish and corresponds directly with the Qabalistic level of Briah which is known as the *creative world*. Again, Olibish is a sphere of creation. The figure representing the level of Olibish is commonly known as Amun Ra. Though typically considered to be an individual deity, Amun Ra here would serve as a symbol of a station or level of creation.

---

[6] D&C 88:6

XLIII. Olibish or Amun Ra operating at the Qabalistic level of Briah.

Three of the qabalistic sephiroth operate within the creative level of Briah: Chesed, Tiphereth and Geburah. While it is not the scope of this writing to detail the attributes of all of the sephiroth, it is relevant to mention that in the Zohar, Abraham is associated with the Sephiroth called Chesed, because he embodies the characteristics of Chesed. Chesed represents mercy with attributes such as "goodness, sharing and love".[7] The wisdom gleaned from Chesed is "Wisdom of Clarity", known as Chokhmah Bahir. Note that clarity is the opposite of the obscurity of mist.[8] Geburah represents justice. Because of Isaac's undeviating obedience to God's commandments, he is associated with the Sephiroth, Geburah. Tiphereth symbolizes the balance between Chesed and Geburah, mercy and justice and symbolizes beauty. Jacob or Israel is associated with Tiphereth. These three sephiroth as symbolized by Abraham, Isaac and Jacob (Israel) are also as the two pillars and keystone in the arch.

Now let's look at the relationship between the Atziluth or Kolob level and the Briah or Olibish level as symbolized by Amun Ra. The level of Kolob would be the place to where the

---

[7] Rosicrucian Digest, Volume 92, Number 1, 2014, pp. 32-37.

[8] 1 Nephi 8:23, 1 Nephi 12:3-4

Lord was fixed that he may ascend above all things and below all things, "that he comprehended all things". All things are present before him. A key to understanding the level of Qabalistic Atziluth or the Kolob level is found in D&C 38:1-3. "Thus saith the Lord your God, even Jesus Christ, the Great I Am, Alpha and Omega, the beginning and the end, the same which looked upon the wide expanse of eternity (Fig. 4), and all the seraphic hosts of heaven before the world was made. The same which

XLIV. Figures 3&7 are masculine and feminine reflections; the two "pillars of Ma'at" as above, so below.

knoweth all things, for all things are present before mine eyes; I am the same which spake, and the world was made, and all things came by me."[9] Here, the Lord is talking of his most high position near Kolob where all things are present before him and he looks upon all the seraphic hosts of heaven; that includes arch angels. We know that Briah is the level where the arch angels reside and angels are characterized by their ability to transition from one level to another. Creation is effectuated by the angels at the command of the Lord. This is where the three higher arch angels reside: Michael, Gabriel and Raphael. These are a reflection

of the Lord and collectively share a unity with him. The level of Olibish is equated with the Hebrew letter Heh. The light propagates from Kolob or the Yod, but it is at the level of Olibish where the plans are conceived by the Lord.

In figure 3, we find Ra or Horus Ra. Joseph Smith interprets Horus Ra to be God sitting on his throne. He wears a "crown of

---

[9] D&C 38:1-3

eternal light upon his head". The crown referred to here is actually a representation of the level of Kolob or Atziluth itself; in particular this would correspond with the Qabalistic *kether*. The Lord is in continual communion with the level of Kolob and can ascend to it. With the Lord operating at the levels of Kolob and Olibish, he is mediating between the angelic hosts and the eternal celestial glory of Kolob. The wide expanse of eternity or space and kingdom over which the law is given is represented on

the opposing side of the hypocephalus in figure 4. To this figure, Joseph assigns the Hebrew name of Raukeeyang. Just as the level of Briah is a reflection of Atziluth in Qabalah, so also Raukeeyang is a reflection of Kolob. Raukeeyang is

XLV. Figure 4 is Raukeeyang or the Egyptian Sokar.

assigned the number 1000, which is really a very key piece of information in number symbolism because the number itself suggests the figure symbolizes the three dimensions of space. So to say that the figure represents the "expanse", is to say that the figure represents the same spatial dimensional properties as Kolob. In spite of Raukeeyang being commonly known in Egyptian culture as Sokar, the figure also takes on the attributes of Nut, whose wings span the heavens in the same manner that we described the wings of Ma'at spanning the diameter of the Chartres labyrinth. We may ask why Joseph is inspired to give this figure a Hebrew name since the other names are presumably Egyptian. In any case, the level of Olibish or Briah is associated with the Hebrew letter Heh.

Level 3: Enish-go-on-dosh and Yetzirah

In Qabalah the level of Yetzirah is known as the *formative world*. This is the level of angelic hosts. When Moroni appears to Joseph Smith once a year for every four years on the day of autumnal equinox, his last cosmic stop before arriving at the Smith farm would presumably have been by the level of Enish-

XLVI. Figure 5 is the Hathor cow and represents the heavenly mediums through which light flows from the presence of God above to his children below.

go-on-dosh or Yetzirah. This realm is represented by the Hathor cow in figure 5. Joseph's explanation states that this is one of the governing planets and cites that the Egyptians considered it to be the Sun, though in Joseph's explanation he refers to it as a planet. It "borrows" its governing light from Kolob through a governing power or medium that Joseph names Kae-e-vanrash. The Greek word from which the word planet derives is *planasthai* and means "wandering". This was because some of the lights in the heavens were not fixed relative to each other, but could move; they seemed to have agency and moved willfully through the rest of the fixed stars. These wanderers may be considered to be either planets or closely related to angels as they move through the heavens.

When the *three* Nephites were transfigured[10], it would be to

---

[10] 3 Nephi 28:15

this level that they were likely raised. They are promised that at a later time they would "receive a greater change, and to be received into the kingdom of the Father to go no more out." The ascension of the three Nephites reveals some more information about the nature of the Qabalistic level of Yetzirah or Enish-go-on-dosh. It is a quasi-state from where angels seem to be able to interact with God's children on Earth to some degree. The idea here is that the angels receive their light from God, in the same analogous manner that the wandering stars receive their light from Kolob; through keys or mediums that is. The total number of planasthai listed in the figure 5 explanation are fifteen. When earth, the moon and the sun are included, the total is eighteen. The level of Enish-go-ondosh or Yetzirah is associated with the Hebrew letter Vau.

Level 4: The Earth in Its Four Quarters and Assiah

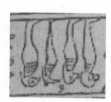

XLVII. Fig. 6 represents the Earth in its four quarters, Adam or the level of material and action known as Assiah.

In Qabalah the level of Assiah is known as the *material world* or the *world of action*. Joseph's explanation of figure 6 explains that the four figures represent "this earth in its four quarters". He doesn't simply say they represent the earth, but specifically the earth in its four quarters. For all of the unity that Kolob represents, the earth in its four quarters is broken apart into its parts. When the ancient goddess, Isis, collected 13 of the 14 body parts of her husband Osiris from across the land; the parts were placed in 4 canopic jars in preparation for a resurrection ceremony. If the spinal column of Osiris represents a ladder, this level is the bottom rung. In the Tree of Jesse window of Chartres, this is where Jesse lies in his bed lamenting his carnal nature; yet it is in Jesse that the ladder that ascends to Christ is rooted.

This is the fallen world we live in and is associated with our bodily appetites and the animal kingdom. It is because of this aspect that it may feasibly be written that "the natural man is an enemy to God, and has been from the fall of Adam".[11] Nevertheless, it is a diffuse and obscured reflection of God. One third of the spiritual posterity of God rebelled and those spirits were cast down to Earth and "it must needs be that the devil should tempt the children of men, or they could not be agents unto themselves".[12] They were one third because they are represented as the third part, the unseen spirits that live below the belt and that entice the spirit to stay attached to the material. In the Egyptian hypocephalus, this is the upside down world, the underworld. If Kolob is numerically symbolized by unity or 1, then earth in its perfected, resurrected, atoned for and celestialized state may be symbolized by the number 10.

Light flows from the creative origin and place of God's dwelling through different mediums down until they reach Adam's posterity. Energy and matter are one.[13] All spirit is matter.[14] All spirit and matter are governed from above by light.[15]

---

[11] Mosiah 3:19

[12] D&C 29:39

[13] Wave-particle duality was defined by DeBroglie as $hv=mc^2$ in his thesis in 1924.

[14] D&C 131:7-8

[15] Cook, M. Garfield, "Science and Modern Revelation", 1981, p. 118

The Microcosm

The way we have looked at the Tree so far is from a macroscopic perspective; we are looking at the whole tree outside of ourselves. This time *we* are the tree. We have looked at this as the great expansive temple of the cosmos with light flowing through all levels. While en route in this journey of thinking, we made note of the Hebrew letters that are associated with each of the four levels which are respectively: Y, H, V, H. Together, these letters constitute the Tetragrammaton and represent the ineffable or "unmouthable" name of God. Some say that it is transliterated against the wish of the Hebrew tradition into the English word so that we can all simply pronounce it without being stoned, Jehovah. This is the name by which we know the Lord in the Old Testament. After Jehova was born into his earthly body, he was given the new name, Jesus. All that is embodied in the hypocephalus and Qabalah is the omniscient, omnipresent and omnipotent functioning of the Spirit of the Lord. Each of us is created in his image. Thusly, this same spiritual architecture that constitutes the Lord's spiritual being is the same that we are made of and so we can look at the same

Level	Number Symbol	Pythagorean Tetractys	Decad Sum	Tetragrammaton	
1	1	Monad	1	Y	י
2	2	Dyad	3	H	ה
3	3	Triad	6	V	ו
4	4	Quaternary	10	H	ה

XLVIII. *Attributes of the four levels of the Tree of Life: Number, Tetractys, Decad Sum, Tetragrammaton. They are compared in the table above and in the next three tables.*

symbols as the parts of a system that is working within us; or rather a system that is us. This time we will look at things from the inside, and let's do so starting from the feet and then on up to the crown.

Level	Priesthood Order After the Most High God	Christ's Church	Book of Abraham, Facsimile 2 (Sheshonq Hypocephalus)	Joseph Smith's Explanation of Book of Abraham, Facsimile 2
1	Elohim (both male and female)	God the Father	Fig. 1,2	Kolob, or the first creation
2	Jehova, Michael	Jesus Christ	Fig. 2,3	Olibish; the place where God resides holding Priesthood keys. God sitting upon his throne crowned with Light
3	Ministering Angels	Peter, James & John (First Presidency)	Fig. 5,7,3	God sitting on his throne, revealing key words of the Priesthood; the sign of the Holy Ghost to Abraham
4	Adam and Eve	Worldwide Church Members	Fig. 6	Represents the Earth in its four quarters.

XLIX. Attributes of the four levels of the Tree of Life: priesthood, church, Book of Abraham Facsimile 2, Joseph Smith explanation of Facsimile 2 They are compared in the table above, the previous table and in the next two tables.

Level 4: Objective Thinking, Nephesh or the Earth in Its Four Quarters

Let's start with the hypocephalus figure 6. There are four beasts that represent the Earth in its four quarters. This is the objective world that we live in. This would best be described as being ruled by the natural man, the sex drive and the basic securities of warmth, shelter and food. Spiritually, one third of God's children were cast down to this level to rule and reign and

Level	Qabalistic Tree of Life	Level of Creation	Qabalistic Tree of Life Sephiroth	Hebrew Alphabet
1	Atziluth	Archetypal, Emanation	1,2,3	All letters combined
2	Briah	Creative	4,5,6	Three Mother Letters
3	Yetzirah	Formative	7,8,9	The Seven Double Letters
4	Assiah	Material, Action	10	The 12 Simple Letters

L. Attributes of the four levels of the Tree of Life: Qabalistic Tree of Life, Level of Creation, Qabalistic Tree of Life Sephiroth, Hebrew Alphabet. They are compared in the table above, the previous 2 tables and in the next table.

tempt us in our bodily experience. This is not the realm of self-reflection but rather of sensual attentiveness. The five objective senses are sight, hearing, smell, taste and touch and are the scope of this sphere of creation. This is the world of objective thinking; here we experience the world with our physical senses. It was to experience this temporal world for which we were born. When Lehi saw the people in the great and spacious building mocking those that held to the iron rod, he saw a part of the world of Assiah. Those stuck in the great and spacious building were separated by a great abyss. This realm is also called in Hebrew, Nehemesh. This is associated with the last H in the tetragrammaton.

Level 3: Subjective Thinking, Ruach
or Enish-go-on-dosh

This is the level of subjective thinking. This is where reason occurs. Before Lehi sees the Tree of Life in his meditation, he first reasons within himself. This is the intellectual level. This is the realm that is governed by Enish-go-ondosh. We are enlightened in this realm by light that flows from Kolob or from cosmic consciousness. This is referred to in Hebrew as Ruach and is associated with the Vau in the tetragrammaton.

Level 2: Subconscious Thinking, Neshamah or Olibish

The level of subconscious thinking is the level that happens in the watery dream states of the mind. Figures 3 and 7 of the hypocephalus show a communication occurring between the Lord and Abraham. In Lehi's meditation he moves from reasoning to dream like vision. It is in this state that he meets a man dressed in a white robe. This is the level of dream symbols. This is where angelic ministrations may occur while we sleep. In the microcosm, the angels are parts of our own psychic being and they work for us in harmony and under the orchestration of the Lord. When we go to bed at night, our minds go to work to repair the fractured thinking of our day. One of the primary functions of dreaming is assimilation of new information. While it feels like it is not actually us making the dream, in fact, it is a part of us or rather many parts of us dissolved in the waters of sleep. It is the angelic work force within; the level where creativity forms the foundation for the next day. Meanwhile as we sleep, the stars wander in the heavens above. A thought that we have today will have an effect within us for about three days. It is the subjective that reconciles the objective with the subconscious. This is also referred to in Hebrew as Neshamah and the letter H in the tetragrammaton.

Level 1: Cosmic Consciousness, Chiah or Kolob

Cosmic consciousness in Mormon terms is really about being in tune with the Holy Ghost. To be in tune with the Holy Ghost is in fact the objective of the mystic. This is the most practical way to understand it. When we humble ourselves and conform our will to the will of the Lord, doing as he leads us to do, we are in fact, acting in behalf of the Lord. We become part of the Lord's orchestration. The light flows in all things and through all things and finds connectivity in this realm. We never truly wear a crown because the crown is a shared resource and belongs only to the Lord. Within us, this is our conscious contact with God. Lehi's dream is an inner spiritual experience for him.

In Lehi's dream, after the man dressed in white visits Lehi, he ascends to the level of the Qabalistic Chiah. It is here that he tastes of the fruit of the Tree of Life. He also looks down towards his family hoping they will hold to the iron rod to also ascend to the level of this celestial sanctum and join him. It truly is a spiritual sanctuary to Lehi and it is available for all to access. What must be realized is that the mocking of the people in the great and spacious building is, therefore, an inner conflict within Lehi and also in each of us. Our own self shaming, if heeded, can distract our celestial focus. It is at this level that in prayer and meditation to God the Father, we may be infused with spiritual light. We may also pray in behalf of others. Our prayers, guided by the Holy Ghost, may be the mind of the Lord and may be the inspiration to another to see through the mists that impede their

Level	Lehi's Dream	Level of Consciousness	Qabalistic Iron Rod
1	All things compound in one (2Ne2:11) The tree and fruit	Cosmic Consciousness	Sephiroth 1
2	Opposition in All Things (2Ne2:11) Mist (Water and Air) v. Iron Rod; Man in White Robe v Dark Dreariness	Subconscious	Sephiroth 6
3	There must needs be an atonement (2Ne2:11) The iron rod extending forth; Man in White Robe v Dark Dreariness	Subjective	Sephiroth 9
4	Men are that they might have joy (2Ne2:25) Mankind on both sides of river, Iron rod extends to one side	Objective	Sephiroth 10

LI. Attributes of the four levels of the Tree of Life: Lehi's Dream, Level of Consciousness, Qabalistic Iron Rod. They are compared in the table above and in the previous 3 tables.

progress towards the Tree of Life. This level is known in Hebrew as Chiah and the letter Y in the tetragrammaton. The four levels of the Tree of Life are thusly represented by the four letters YHVH or Yod Heh Vau Heh.

Much more can be explored in this comparison between the Egyptian hypocephalus and the Qabalah when considered through the context of Lehi's Dream. Joseph Smith's interpretation of the Sheshonq hypocephalus is accurate enough and gives enough information to successfully make the comparison. The descriptions of the Tree of Life after the tradition of Lehi are given by three seers and mystics: Lehi, Nephi and Alma. They are seers because they see spiritually. They are mystics because they see through the mist into the mysteries. To some degree, we may consider that there is a Tree of Light and a Tree of Love that are different the one from the other just as the intellectual mind is distinguished from the emotional heart. To find the key and hold to the balance between the two yield the fruit of the third, the Tree of Life.

The Interface

The interface may be thought of as that which makes at one the ineffable two undivided faces of Kolob, so to speak, the two faces of Janus, the two principles of Ma'at, the keystone in the arch that unites the two pillars, the vesica piscis that unites two circles and the eternal cosmic stitching effectuated by the atonement of Jesus Christ. It is the liminal zone where our microcosm is stitched to the macrocosm, where the esoteric is at one with the exoteric. Let's look at some arcane and ancient expressions of a few things that happen at the interface.

Forty Days in the Wilderness

The Qabalistic Tree of Life consists of four levels and may be expanded and considered as Four Trees or 16 levels. Four sections of four levels each. We won't pursue this in great detail. Four Qabalistic Trees convey the same essential message as the basic 4 levels; the difference being that it's total number is 4 raised to the power of 2, and may be well said to be four squared. The total number of Sephiroth would be 10 Sephiroth at each level times 4 levels or 40. 40 tends to be a numeric symbol for a period of passing through the wilderness, making a personal sacrifice to the Lord in search of illumination. The path of the children of Israel was to walk 40 years through the desert, making sacrifices unto the Lord, until they reached Mount Sinai where Moses ascended to the mount. He then spent 40 days until he received the tablets written by the *finger of god*. In the Hebrew tradition, it is counseled that the study of Zohar and Kaballah should not start until one is married and over the age of 40. The Brother of Jared, when preparing barges to cross the sea, sought the Lord for help to light the barges for he knew that the Lord had said they "must be encompassed about by the floods". He went to the mount Shelem "and did molten out of a rock 16 small stones; and they were white and clear, even as transparent as glass". While in prayer Jared speaks to the Lord saying, "And I know, O Lord, that thou hast all power, and can do whatsoever thou wilt for the benefit of man; therefore touch these stones, O Lord, with the finger, and prepare them that they may shine forth in darkness; and they shall shine forth unto us in the vessels which we have prepared, that we may have light while we shall cross the sea."[16] The veil is then parted between Jared and the Lord and the Lord extends his finger through the veil to touch and illuminate the 16 stones. The 16 stones having received light from the finger of the Lord act in the precise likeness as Enish-go-on-dosh or the Egyptian Hathor cow as described in fig. 5 of the hypocephalus. In Hebrew, 'Yod', the first letter of the tetragrammaton, literally means "the hand of God" or "the finger of God". Another, example of a man passing through this time of darkness is Jesus himself, Jehovah incarnate. Jesus fasted for forty days. During that time, Lucifer came to him tempting him on three occasions. Each time Jesus is faced with a temptation or trial, he prevails with a response bearing wisdom. In fact, Lucifer suggests that Jesus use his power to turn stones into bread, but Jesus will not, for it is not by bread alone that man shall live, thusly it is not bread that is desired from the stones, but the word of God. Thusly the stones remain stones and it is for the word of God that Jesus is seeking. Jesus is then challenged to exploit angels to serve him for the sake of impressive miracles that would seem to have no effect other than to evoke pride or envy. Jesus declines to jump off of a wall. Interesting proposal by Lucifer since there was likely no guarantee that Jesus would be reared up in any physical way. That would have been bad. Jesus then follows Lucifer up a high mountain, as occurred with Moses and with the Brother of Jared and many other men. Lucifer, though leading Jesus physically higher to view a physical kingdom, requests of Jesus to go to him for governing direction, to the prince of darkness. Jesus again responds to the trial with an act of wisdom and no longer takes the hooks. Jesus then casts out Lucifer. It appears that Jesus is on the mountain top and it is

---

[16] Ether 3:4

at this point he has a visitation by angels. Unfortunately the first thing that happens after he has this experience is that John the Baptist is then taken prisoner. When the flood of water came upon the earth in the days of Noah it rained for 40 days. After the mountain tops were seen it was 40 days until Noah opened the window in his ark. After the raven is sent forth to dry the land, the dove is sent forth three times, Noah departs from the ark to find of all things luminescent and beautiful, the art work of the Lord. By bringing water and air together, even as the veils that divide the heavens and earth as clouds, even as the mist surrounding the Tree of Life, the mists and moisture in the air act as prisms as numerous as the silicon sand of the seas; the white light from the sun is then diffracted by the varying *angles* of incidence, as it were the work of *angels* of incidents, bringing to the eyes of Noah a sure confirmation that the seas of aqueous wilderness have been crossed.

So as the words of the stories may dissolve in time, yet in the ether the numbers remain fixed and sure. 4 levels squared are 16. To journey the paths requires passing through veils, and as Lehi passed through a dark and dreary wilderness, so did others seeking illumination of the Lord. On the Salt Lake City Temple there is a stone symbol. It is a sun with 40 rays extending outward. If we consider the Egyptian motif where each of the rays is as a hand extending from the celestial pavilions of the Lord to help he or she who must pass through the dark and dreary wilderness, we may then consider each of those rays as the hand of a guide dressed in white reaching out to the hand of the initiate to carry them through the dark and dreary abyss that divides man from the sephirotic paths of celestial light. Jupiter, as a barge that carries Horus across the watery night skies, serves the same saving purpose as the extended hands of mercy. Jesus the Christ sacrificed in the wilderness of dryness before meeting angels. Their time is 40 days and 40 years.

A Jupiter Talisman: Emanations of Light Written in Symbols

"Math is the study of patterns."
–Mr. Matlack (My high school math teacher)

The Book of Abraham Facsimile 2 contains hieroglyphs that were on an Egyptian papyrus that came into the possession of Joseph Smith. It is also known as the hypocephalus of Sheshonq.[17] Hypocephalae were known to have been placed under the head of the dead as a guide for the spirit's journey through the cosmos to eternal life, as well as man's place in it during life. A hypocephalus is thought to have been custom-made by the person using it. Each is similar in function, but differ in specifics. The Book of Abraham Facsimile 2 may be considered to be a sort of talisman in addition to its funerary function. By reading through the figures, we are following through a sequence of ideas. An overall picture of the cosmos is revealed and the figures seed the mind to receive further revelation on the subjects presented. Let's hypothesize that the device referred to as the "Joseph Smith Jupiter Talisman" is not too different in its purposes except that whereas the hypocephalus details a map of the entire cosmos and man's

---

[17] Michael D. Rhodes, "The Hor Book of Breathings, A Translation and Commentary", 2002, The Foundation for Ancient Research and Mormon Studies, p. 2.

journey of ascension through it, the Jupiter Talisman acquaints its user with some of the smaller spiritual job descriptions found within the great cosmic organization. In other words, it contains symbols that represent the spirit of something or essence of the attributes of one specific function within the overall model of the hypocephalus. Another way of examining this, assuming the hypocephalus and Sefer Yezirah are equivalent in purpose, it may be reasoned that each of the individual Qabalistic Sephiroth of the Sefer Yetzirah and the Tree of Sephiroth are embedded in some fashion and to some degree within the hypocephalus.

The Jupiter talisman contains information representing that spirit or essence of an angelic roll or function in numerical symbols or in their Hebrew lettering equivalents. It is like a slice of the pie whereas the hypocephalus is the whole cosmological pie. One geometric commonality is that the talisman and the hypocephalus are designed as rounds or circles filled with smaller squares and the figures are not read linearly. Each of the squares contains symbols that convey information. The Jupiter talisman includes a sigil which is the key that reveals the sequence in which the number symbols or Hebrew letters ought to be recollected. The sigil then becomes a mapping and a summary of the number symbols and may be used for quick recollection. That's the gist of it anyhow. It would be incomplete to not mention that practioners of talismanic magic kinesthetically make the sign or sigil in the air as an invocation of the principles embodied in the symbols of the talisman. The hypocephalus does not come with a sigil, however, Joseph Smith provided a sequence to the figure explanations that acts in the same manner as a sigil.

By referring back to Lehi's vision of the Tree of Life, we can take a look at the Abraham Facsimile 2 hypocephalus and see how the Joseph Smith Jupiter talisman is related to the ascension symbolism and carries meaning.

Angels of Transition

Let's refer back to Abraham Facsimile 2, figure 3 depiction of God in his throne. At the back end of the Egyptian barge, the oar extends from the air above the barge to the water below the barge. This part of the symbol in this context symbolizes governance or navigation upon the waters of Nun. Nun, the male principle of primeval waters or the dark and dreary abyss of creation, carries the solar barque.[18] The oar extends from water to air. Indeed the rear end of the boat with oar positioned as it is appears to be the same shape as the astrological symbol for Jupiter. The convex and concave aspects of the barque serve to symbolize the bounds of the universe which are modeled in the Egyptian temple.[19] At first, this seems entirely unlikely since the symbol for Jupiter is derived from geometric symbolism and the end of the boat in the hypocephalus appears to likely be just the plain and simple back end of a boat or barge. However, in this case we are doing an intuitive contemplation; let's follow an intuitive consideration of this interesting shape at the end of the barge. Interestingly, this symbol for Jupiter represents the mind arising over the horizon of matter as represented by the cross in the same manner that Horus traverses the sky in his barque each

---

[18] Wilkinson, Richard H., "The Complete Gods and Goddesses of Ancient Egypt", 2003, Thames and Hudson, Inc., p. 117.

[19] Ibid, p.118.

day. This is a confirming thought and is a key point! It is a symbol of transition and change.

Staying with the essence of the symbol we note that the path of Lehi in his vision ascends over the material things of the world. He falls asleep to material things in order to awaken to greater spiritual things. Lehi earnestly seeks God and passes through darkness and dreariness to eventually be taken in by the love and mercy of God. (In that dream, the dark and dreary waste may play the same function as the waters of Nun.) Now, to take this concept and refer back to the Hebrew number and letter gematria system, we recall that the attribute of love and sharing, typified by mercy, is represented by Chesed. Chesed is one of the emanations of light or Sephiroth in the hermetic Qabalah. Strikingly confirming of this relationship is the fact that the Jupiter talisman is commonly associated with the very virtue of mercy or Chesed. When Christ extends his hand to Peter to draw him from the water back into the air and walk on water with Christ in the fourth watch, Peter, like Lehi ascending above material temptation and passing through a water-air veil, is the acted upon by Chesed qualities. Like the oar in the barque, Peter himself is halfway in the water and halfway in the air.

Passing through this veil by the hand of mercy (Chesed) of the Lord seems to be symbolized by the barque. Let's take particular interest in the oar aspect of the symbol again. It extends from air to water and the boat acts as a veil between the two, or the action at the interface between the two. The etymological origin of the word oar is the Old English word *ar* and Proto-Germanic *airo*. The Latin word, *aerum,* means the atmosphere or sky. *Ar* is used as a root in the word *artery* and *aorta* meaning "that which lifts" or rises. That right there is the link in the iconography between the hypocephalus figure 3,

Lehi's ascent through the dark and dreary waste or mist, Peter's ascension out of the waters in the fourth watch and is thusly the intended function of the Joseph Smith Jupiter talisman evocation. The Old English *ar* is also the etymological origin of *ore*. It is by the ore of the iron rod that Lehi, Nephi and family ascend above the mists. Oar and *rower* are thought to be related in Old English and the word *crown* contains the root *row*. Joseph Smith clarifies that figure 3 is made to represent God on his throne "with a crown of eternal light upon his head". Gold is symbolic of wisdom and the root *aur* for gold is also obviously the same sound as *or* and *ore* and *oar*. The Gnostics used the crown to symbolize light and referred to it as *or*.[20]

LII. *St. Apollonaris window at Chartres Cathedral. Oar has handle that appears as a golden tau. Photo courtesy of Dr. Stuart Whatling, PhD.*

Let's refer back to symbols found in the Chartres cathedral and find out with what new insight we may be endued. The darkness of the heavens are symbolized as the Waters of Nun, thusly bodies navigating through the heavens may be considered to move upon the waters of space and represent a godly

---

[20] Bayley, Harold, "The Lost Language of Symbolism".

transcendence. In the Chartres stained glass window of St. Apollinaris in the boat, the oar has a golden handle that is shaped like the Tau. The tau is a symbol of transition and also of the vernal equinox.[21] The orientation of the boat is precisely analogous to figure 3 of Fac. 2. In figure 3 there are three depictions of Horus! There is the eye of Horus looking forward, there is the eye of Horus looking backward, and there is the physical and present Horus representation in the center; which in itself, as a set of symbols, is a reflection of the Janus motif found in figures 1 and 2. (That concept is worth a solemn contemplation.) In the St. Apollinaris window, the oarsman in green sits at the back of the boat and is looking forward, the front man in red is looking back toward the central figure who is fully robed wearing both red and green.

The symbol structure and motif is so strikingly similar to the point that I have to wonder if the French-Gaulish families of the Merovingian and Carolingian Dynasty eras may have had Egyptian papyrus in their possession as far back as 1260 A.D. A review of the genealogies printed by Nicholas De Vere implies that it would be entirely possible that European families had Egyptian documents in their possession.[22] Not only because they could receive them from Egypt through archaeological extractions, but because they are genealogically related to Egyptians in part through their Merovingian lineage.

Thinking back to the stained glass window of St. Apollinaris, while one would expect motion from a boat, the St. Apollinaris window suggests that the boat may not physically be

---

[21] Brown, Robert, "Stellar Theology and Masonic Astronomy", Health Research Books, 1996 edition, p.99.

[22] Nicholas DeVere, "Dragon Legacy", 2004, The Book Tree Publishing, p. 408.

moving in spite of appearing to be in a state of much dynamic nautical activity. Suggesting this, the sail of the boat has the Tau symbol embedded in the mast which is a symbol of balance. Here is the astounding irony! The wind or air in the sail is blowing in direct opposition to the direction that the oarsman appears to be rowing in the water. (To yet again reiterate, mist is the combination of both air and water which exists in a balance of conditions.) All of the hard work of the oarsman in rowing is countered by the blowing wind that fills the sail. The handle of the oar is also inconspicuously depicted as a Tau symbol. The Tau symbol being on both the oar and in the sail in gold demonstrates that there is opposition that the navigators encounter, yet balance may be maintained between the force generated by the oar in water in opposition to the force of air and wind. The two Tau symbols in the window yield the Ma'at and Thoth companionship that brings balance. So, the Ma'at and Thoth theme are discernible in figure 1, figure 2 and figure 3. They are discernible below in figure 7 of the hypocephalus as the compass and square. Joseph Smith's explanation of figure 3 is that the central figure is clothed with power and wears a crown. Typically the crown and gold symbolize perfection and the Horus-God figure wears the crown that is the sun.

In the St. Apollinaris window, the Apollinaris figure is wearing a crown or cap. This type of cap became well known as the papal miter and is the shape of a fish mouth. The golden tau shaped handle in the hands of the oarsman is a symbol that seems to be a reflection of the tau shape in the mast above. In the hypocephalus, in fig. 7, which again is a lower reflection of fig.3, the throne itself has the lower body of the fish, which further demonstrates the connection in symbols. St. Apollinaris has in his hand a book and as books do contain words, so too does the Horus-god bear the grand key-words. The three men in the barge are a symbolic analog of Horus and the two wedjat eyes in fig. 3. This symbolic triad may be considered to represent three of the Sephiroth in the hebrew Qabalistic Tree of Life. At the Atziluth level they are Kether (Crown), Binah (Understanding), Chokmah(Wisdom). The Sephiroth in Qabalah that connects the lower level to the highest level is called Chesed or mercy.

Looking more closely at this triad of the barge in the St. Apollinaris window, let's observe the similarity with the hypocephalus symbols of figure 3. The work of the oarsman produces one force that relies on water in opposition to the forces of wind that blow in the other direction. He is cloaked in green, covering what I assume to be very long hair and employs water to produce a motive force. His hands are closed, holding to the gold tau oar handle. The front man in the boat has tonsured hair, he is cloaked in red and is upwind, or in the direction from where the wind blows in this depiction. His hand is open and in the air. The water to air interface acts as a veil and the oar seems to represent the medium by which one interacts through the veil. This archetype has its analog in the relationship of Horus of figure 3 interacting through various veils of symbol and geometry with Enish-go-on-dosh, the Hathor Cow. In another Egyptian funeral papyrus, that of Amonemsaf, we find Horus' head descending below the barge to peer into the underworld [23] through the medium of 15 stars, just as Joseph Smith describes of the Hathor cow's function as a medium of light in the fig. 5 explanation. Thusly the Hathor cow partially represents the work

---

[23] Hugh Nibley and Michael D. Rhodes, "One Eternal Round", 2010, p. 296.

that is done on earth that helps keep things in balance; the duties of the Priesthood. Let me emphasize the importance of the nature of priesthood service, for it is a labor of love. Only by love unfeigned, kindness, meekness, gentleness, patience and longsuffering may the work be led (D&C 121: 34-46). This is the proper manner to lead a righteous and obedient cow to work. Thusly the church is indeed, at times, somewhat like a cow, respectfully. It moves forward to bring spiritual milk or light to the four quarters of the earth. This connection between the objective world we live in and the upper archetypal levels where Horus operates to maintain balance is akin to the path way in Hebrew Qabalah that leads to the level of Atziluth, and is only entered in the way that Lehi approached the Tree of Life; for it was after all he could do by living the law, that in the end of that faithful approach to the tree he was taken by the hand of mercy. Again, this mercy is considered in Qabalah to be a Sephiroth called Chesed and it is the way by which one may proceed towards the Tree of Life after all he can do to live justly; towards the triad that is Kether, Chokmah and Binah.

In the story of a boy named Siddartha who, like Icarus, ascends too high in his ambitions, pursuits and even successes, finds himself lying at the side of a river after his life has fallen apart. While by the river a man raises him from his fallen state and employs him as an oarsman on a raft to take people across the river. In this work of helping others cross the waters he discovers what wisdom really is. He himself is metaphoric of an initiator. The apprentice becomes the master as he helps others cross the abyss.[24]

---

[24] Hesse, Hermann, "Siddhartha", Shambhala Publications.

LIII.   Hypochephalus at British Museum, London, England. Photo by author, 2010.

The planet Jupiter is known as the son of the Sun. In Babylonian astronomy, Jupiter is known as *Niburu*.[25] It is also called in the Akkadian language *Niburu* and literally means "ferry boat" or "transition point". Ferry boats carry people across a river or body of water. In the hypocephalae I saw at the British Museum, barques act as ferry boats that transition souls between the worlds.[26]

---

[25] "The Assyrian Dictionary of the Oriental Institute of the University of Chicago",
Volume 11, N, part II, page 145.

[26] Nibley, Hugh, "The Message of the Joseph Smith Papyrii", 2005, Deseret Book, p.223.

In Lehi's dream he saw a man dressed in a white robe that carried him into a dreary wasteland. Earlier we referred to this man as performing the same work as the iron rod; we may now, with respect to crossing through the dark and dreary wasteland, consider him symbolically to be like Jupiter. When Lehi called to the Lord, it was mercy that delivered him. Thusly Jupiter is also a symbol of mercy in the sense that mercy helps us cross the abyss to the Tree of Life.

Jupiter also symbolizes Osiris. Jupiter crosses the winter solstice, traveling from the end to the beginning from the Omega to the Alpha.

LIV. Another hypocephalus on display at the British Museum, London, England. Photo by author, 2010.

We can well confirm that the attribute of Chesed and the esoteric attributes of Jupiter are thusly connected in symbolic meaning, but in particular they conduct the same essence.

Jupiter and the Barges of the Brother of Jared

The 8 barges of the Brother of Jared were lit by 16 stones. The square root of 16 is 4. Conversely, 4 squared is 16. Thusly, the symbol of the barge or ferry that helps the sons of God cross the watery abyss is wonderfully equivalent to the symbols of Jupiter or Chesed. The numeric symbols appropriately assigned to the Jupiter barge symbol would be 4 squared. Geometrically this could be represented by a 4 x 4 square, consisting of 16 unit squares.

The Square and Number

The square is a perfect geometric symbol. Each of its sides is equivalent in length to each other. Another symbol of Jupiter or the barge is the Hathor Cow. And the Hathor cow is depicted as having 16 star shaped bosoms, from which light propagates, flowing forth as the milk of a cow, which then flows to the four sons of Horus or four quarters of the earth. It's astounding to find that the number of stones of light prepared by the Lord and the Brother of Jared is the same as the number of stars on the Hathor cow. It is also the number of planets described by Joseph Smith in Fac. 2 explanation of the figure 5 Hathor Cow; Enish-go-on-dosh is the governing planet over 15 other planets for a total of 16. The square relationship between 4 and 16 is clearly present in the hypocephalae. When comparing the Abraham hypocephalus to those found in the British Museum, it becomes even more clear that equivalency between the barge and Hathor cow is present, though represented by different symbols at different levels. The 4 sons of Horus partake of the milk or wisdom of the 16 bosoms of the cow, or however you want to say that.

Let's consider and build on the idea that these heavenly bodies described in the hypocephalus do as Pythagorean thought suggests; they hum. Let's go with the idea that light, which modernly may be considered to be energy or vibration, may pass through these symbolic and hypothetical planets analogous to how essence and spirit flow through number. This planetary light medium could then be represented mathematically and geometrically as a 4 x 4 matrix of numbers.

The word *matrix* heralds from *matre* or mother. The mattress also heralds from matre. And the friend of the mattress is the *pillow*, which heralds from common origins as pillar; like Jacob's stone that became a pillar that he rested his head on. Each unit square of the 4x4 matrix can be assigned a number. Just a caution in thinking here, in the same manner we put the days in the squares in our calendar yet the reality is that there is continual fluence in time, so too, the squaring of these numbers is our human and finite effort to contain the symbols that truly represent a variety of essences that are not finite, but rather of a light that is in all things and through all things, ever reconstituting from one state to the next as expressed in number. In the physical geometric sense the length of each side of the square is equivalent. In Hebrew gematria, when the sum of four numbers is equal to the sum of four different numbers, their sums carry similar meanings. They are archetypal. So just like each of the four sides is equal in length so too may this geometric symbolic meaning be carried to the number symbols. Thusly the gematric values of the sides of the matrix can be said to be square also.

The square is a symbol of physical manifestation. In fact, numbers may be placed so that all of the horizontal rows, all of the vertical columns and the major diagonals are equal to the same sum number. It implies wholeness. Since Egyptian numbers did not include zero, assignment of numbers should likely start with the first integer natural number which is 1 and the matrix should contain no zero values. 4 x4 =16 so the natural integers 1 through 16 are assigned such that the gematric sums in the horizontal and vertical are equivalent. It may be repeated that each number has a Hebrew equivalent, the meanings of words or names constructed from the horizontals and verticals have equivalency in archetypal meaning. In the western esoteric tradition, names found in the matrix of numbers or rather in their letter equivalents are assigned to angels. It seems that the angels that were involved with the creation of Earth would have thusly been inextricably associated with certain numeric sequences and the essence or spiritual "notes" associated with them. As it would be hard to believe any individual spirit son or daughter of God would be inextricably tied to a number, perhaps one may consider the angel to be a calling or a position just like the vocal part of a choir. As we mentioned earlier, the pattern traced from letter to letter of the name found in the matrix is called the "sigil". The word sigil comes from the Latin word *sigillum*, which means "sign". The numeric matrix, with its accompanying name and sigil when placed on a round piece of metal is called a "talisman". The word talisman comes from

Arabic *tilsam* which derives from the Greek *telos*. Another word for such a talisman could be *token* which derives from Old English *tacen* meaning a sign, symbol or "an evidence". The Old Norse *teikn* also means zodiac sign. There are four cardinal *zodiac signs.*

Symbols Are Used for Remembering

After the death of Joseph Smith a small coin came forth from the husband of Emma Smith Bidamon. The coin was said to have been in possession of Joseph Smith. It is referred to as a Jupiter talisman and is the talisman we've been discussing. The root of the word talisman is said to have come from the Greek root, *teleo* through the Arabic word *telasm*. This is the same root as found in the words telephone, teleotes and telestial or pertaining to earth. It has engravings on both sides that are of symbolic significance. While these engravings are an entirely foreign numeric and symbolic language to the world at large, to those that have studied ancient symbolism of numbers and the Qabalistic model of the cosmos, these inscriptions may be meaningful. There are a few beliefs regarding the intended use of the talisman. In a simple sense it may be said to have been used for recollection. In the same way a university physics student is permitted by a professor to record the symbols that represent Maxwell's equations of electromagnetism on a 3" x 5" note card for quick recollection during an exam, the coin that Joseph possessed contained symbols that may be used for improved recollection of eternal principles that may be considered to be relevant to the doctrines of the ancient priesthood. Our human minds are capable of memorizing and recalling immense amounts of information if we use an organizational method for "chunking" information. We can remember up to about 6 or 7 digits easily, let's say 7 as in a traditional American telephone number. If we further remember that for each digit 1 through 7 there are 7 digits assigned to each, we are then creating 7x7 or 49 place holders for information. I have tried this method of memorization while in college and it does work well. I was able to write long essays before an essay exam and recover the information in entirety during the exam. Like anything it takes work; memorization work.

Angels, Chesed and Jupiter

The coin that Joseph had is one of several such coins that were made for this type of recollection purpose. Each one may be intended to represent a particular attribute symbolized in numbers.

In the most practical application, a talisman is intended to help the mind disregard the non-essential things that don't pertain to the attribute of interest and to consider the immense and vast possibilities of the creative world. Whether symbolic or literal, the attribute symbolized on

4	14	15	1
9	7	6	12
5	11	10	8
16	2	3	13

LV. The number matrix representing the 4th Sephiroth, Jupiter and Chesed as associated with Abraham. The numbers in this square are found on the Joseph Smith Jupiter talisman in Hebrew.

the coin is also associated with a planet. In particular this coin that was said to have been Joseph's is called a "Jupiter talisman".

Its markings are well known and well published within the world of such curious things and the mathematical labor put into developing the numeric symbols is not unintelligible or without foundation.

As an analogy of its use, it seems that if there were 8 different notes that are being played on a piano simultaneously and we were able to tune into one of the notes while disregarding the other non-essential notes, we could then hear that one singular note and feel its harmony within us. Now, further elaborating upon the analogy, consider that each of these notes were as the singing voice[27] of an angel; one could imagine from beyond the veil our ancient ancestors are employed in the great work of God, charged with admonitions to sing forth to the earth. Imagine that rather than hearing a literal sound of musical harmony coming through the veil, there is a spiritual harmony or note being sung forth. Alma says, "Oh that I were an angel, that I might have the wish of my heart, that I might go forth and speak with the trump of God…as with the voice of thunder."[28] Alma recognized that the voice of angels permeate the earth and act upon the hearts of men and women. He also recognized that he, as a man, was not qualified to interfere with their work. Likely because he knew that the powers of heaven cannot be controlled or handled anymore than we would try to row a boat by handling the oar from underneath the boat. If we try that, we find ourselves, like Peter, underwater. In fact, as a man, Alma could not do this particular work of an angel, God wouldn't permit it.

---

[27] Alma 32:22,23

[28] Alma 29:1,2

A careful analysis of Lehi's dream upon the moment that Lehi is left alone in the dreary wasteland reveals a process for spiritual ascension. What the inner workings of the process are is not as important as knowing the process works. When Lehi is meditating, he envisions a man in a white robe who comes and stands before Lehi and bids Lehi to follow him, let's consider for a moment hypothetically that this man in the white robe is in fact Lehi. In Gestalt psychology, the whole of something is viewed in terms of its parts. Often when we have a dream, the parts of the dreams are parts of us. Applying this logic to Lehi's dream, it is a part of Lehi that comes to another part of Lehi and takes him to a dreary waste. Lehi patiently endures the discomfort of the darkness and dreariness, he didn't start re-writing the story in his mind, he didn't succumb to the aversion the mind would produce to distract one from pain or suffering; he endured the putrefaction. It does not specifically say whether the man in the white robe leaves or stays with Lehi, however, when Lehi's conversation turns to the Lord, the dream symbols change! Lehi prayed for mercy and he was given mercy. The active agent of mercy may itself be considered to be an angel or it may be reasonably said that the Lord sent an angel of mercy to Lehi. The angel isn't characterized by visual appearance or bodily vestiture, but rather the roll of dispensation or *dispensing* that the angel plays; the dispensing and effectuation of mercy. To require description of bodily vestiture be assigned to an angel in order to be considered an angel, would be the requirement of the materially minded. The whole experience is spiritual and occurs within Lehi's mind. The angel or *hand of mercy* may be considered to be the active principle of Chesed, having been extended as the *hand* of the Lord. The man dressed in the white robe, is no longer a component in the dream as a separate part;

Lehi and the man in the white robe become alchemically unified; they always were both Lehi. This transmutation can only occur under the *atoning* power of the Lord; meaning that two parts are made whole or healed! This would be a sort *coniunctio*. Lehi's roll as he leaves Jerusalem also changes. The days of forecasting destruction end, and the days of creating begin; it is the beginning of a new time to build his family and a temple in a new land. The transformation of the dream from waste to a spacious field is in fact the resultant transformation of the work of the angel of mercy (Chesed) sent by the Lord. The landscape of Lehi's mind is undergoing transformation and regeneration. We may expect when one dream symbol departs, it is never destroyed, but transmutated. Thusly, the white robed man dies as to one form, but reappears in the dream as the white fruit of the tree. It may be reasonably suspected that the man in the white robe could be equated with the Sephiroth, Geburah, Mars, or strength, justice and rigor.

Lehi is not alone in his experience. His traditional forebearer, Abraham, also has an experience where the Lord sends forth an angel of mercy, Chesed, to cause a transformation to come upon Abraham as he suffers the dreary and dark moment of contemplation upon the sacrifice of his son Isaac. Eventually, the Lord sends an angel, who then instructs Abraham to release Isaac. The dispensation of mercy upon Abraham is what earns him symbolic equivalence with Chesed.

Joseph Smith gave specific instructions that he felt were important for the general church membership to know regarding communications from angels and interaction with them. Joseph gives three "grand keys" used to discern and qualify angelic ministration by an experiment of faith that can be conducted should an angel appear.[29] The use of the phrase "grand keys" hearkens back to Joseph's interpretations of the Abraham Facsimile 2. His recommendation is to invite the angel to shake hands. There are two kinds of angels that are good, and one third kind that is only deception. The good kinds are either resurrected and have a body of flesh or are not resurrected and do not have a body of flesh. The two kinds are real. The resurrected angel may shake hands as one man shakes hands with another and the experience is objectively tangible. The spirit angel has no body and plays by the rules; he or she will pass on the offer. The third kind doesn't play by the rules, doesn't respect boundaries or covenants and will respond or obey by attempting to shake hands, but cannot because he or she has no body. In this explanation, Joseph made no mention of the use of talismans. The veils that separate man from God were well understood by Joseph and he seems to have felt and was inspired by the Lord that perhaps any one of us could likely have the opportunity to work with angels.

After Moses left the earth, the higher priesthood was taken with him, but the lesser remained, "which priesthood holdeth the key to ministering of angels and the preparatory gospel".[30] Therefore, logic would conclude that since Aaron was ordained by an angel at 8 days old, this would have been done by a resurrected angel, a man ordained of God and having a body of flesh and bone. In comparison with the magnitude of angelic experience Joseph has had, implied in D&C 129, the use of a talisman would have been a trivial tool in his toolbox of spiritual technologies.

---

[29] D&C 129:1-9

[30] D&C 84:26

Of Magi, Seers and Masters

It is commonly said that it was three magi that visited the Christ child at his birth in Bethlehem. They are often referred to as magi and in this singular instance in mainstream Christianity the word magi seems to be well accepted and quite reasonable. The funny thing about it is that the moment you add the letter 'c' to the end of the root word *magi*, we all get quite suspicious and we think of the trickery and deception of "magicians" and rightly so. However, the word "magi" comes from the Persian word *magus* or Greek *magos* and refers to a member of the priesthood. It came onto the European scene in the 1200's. Though the mysteries of God are given to us to explore as each of us has capacity to receive them[31], there is still a modern traditional hesitancy to use the word magi as proper nomenclature for one who does so[32]. The work of the magi in the best sense of the role was to receive and dispense wisdom, light and knowledge; this is essentially the role of a prophet.[33] This is why they may be said to have been the wise men that visited Christ at his birth. They followed the star over Bethlehem. If one stops to consider how it is that wise men can ascertain the location of the birth of a baby that they really know little about by following a star, we must then consider that the spiritual practices of the ancient followers of Christ may have included much more advanced spiritual technologies than we may typically even have the capacity to consider in our busy lives.

---

[31] 1 Nephi 10:18,19

[32] Jacob 4:8,9

[33] See "Magi" in Bible Dictionary, LDS scriptures.

So it is that the Jupiter talisman that may have been in the possession of Joseph Smith contains symbols that help the intellect recall eternal principles in an ordered and methodical way, similar to the way we recall equations for light in physics from the fundamental equations of physics and how they work together. And from what I can discern, the methodology of properly using a talisman for recollection requires a fair amount of intellect if you could find reasonable information on its use in the first place. It is only as magical as the act of remembering. A TV remote control is true magic. Had someone demonstrated the use of a TV remote control in the wrong crowd in Europe in the 1500's, they might have been burned at the stake simply for changing the channel to watch a different football game. My point is that the one thing we can be sure of is that these talismans were used to invoke thoughts within the individual. Thoughts and that call down information from God.

We all have great capacity to nourish the godly attributes that are within each of us. We are fortunate to live in a time where these good and godly attributes can be found in people all around us, if we look diligently and appreciate the variety and diversity amongst us. As we strive to find the people that Divine Orchestration guides us to and to us and emulate their attributes, we may find those attributes growing within ourselves. In times of history, where darkness reigned, it may have been nearly impossible to find certain godly attributes in one's vicinity, and one's theurgic invocations to God may have called down the powers of heaven to instill attributes such as love and mercy.

Cultural influence is profoundly powerful as some of us may have experienced and become aware of. As we read the news or watch trends in behavior, we see trends and norms take form and then dissipate just in the manner that weather comes and goes.

In our daily lives, we are inundated with a chaotic influx of information. Some of it is true and some of it is false. At night, as we sleep, our subconscious integrates the information we receive. As we strive to become more balanced in our daily lives, remembering the basics is helpful. We need sleep, food, water, oxygen, exercise, warmth and the basics of life. If we forget these things our lives may go out of balance. It is helpful to join with others striving to live in harmony with the laws upon which Divinity is predicated, so that we may remember balance. Some participate in a sacrament to remember the divine power of healing. The Lord helps us prevail over the chaos that surrounds us by establishing a pattern for conveying eternal truths; a method for ordering our thinking.

As the doctrines of the ancient priesthood were largely lost, scattered and misunderstood in the centuries following the life of Jesus Christ, pieces were indeed found and they contained fragments of truth. Many honest, hardworking faithful servants of the Lord worked to piece truth together and were successful in many areas. I believe these men and women were at the foundation of the Age of Enlightenment and the Restoration. Whether through the traditional rites of the Freemasons, through one of the many Christian denominations, or passed on through secluded alchemists such as Nicholas Flamel or by way of the simple boy that pulls the plough, we find that virtues, principles, truths, allegories, history, love, life and light were passed on to us; they've flowed like rivers of light to us and they are all around us. Brigham Young and Joseph Smith as well as other Mormon prophets have admonished the latter-day saints to seek out knowledge in the best books. We may then assimilate what we encounter in our studies with what we fundamentally know. As the base of the Great Pyramid at Giza has four cornerstones, or as any gothic cathedral has four cornerstones, there is one that is the Chief Cornerstone. It is relative to the orientation established by the Chief Cornerstone that we may lay a sure foundation and upon that foundation build the temple of our mind. Whether we build with math, economics, art, psychology, philosophy, business, athletics, all of these truths, knowledge and arts may be circumscribed into one great whole. And so, upon the Chief Cornerstone our foundation is established. We find balance in a well rounded circumference of knowledge and application. We may find valuable truth in all things, if we are willing to look for it; leaving what we cannot use behind, yet taking what is for us.

The Jupiter talisman has 16 squares and the 16 numbers may represent the governance of goodness by light and persuasion on the one hand; the merciful hand of God.

With obedience to God's laws come blessings of prosperity. Yet, in opposition, there must be recognized the warning that with prosperity comes the force of pride. Lehi saw a great and spacious building and those that were in it were in the attitude of mocking. This great and spacious building is, in a sense, an opposing force of mercy and the humility to which mercy is extended. Those that hold to the iron rod will still experience its influence. If the mocking voices are heard coming from the great and spacious building, we may take it as a special message; it is the message that it is time to let go of the burning building. As Lehi sat in meditation with the dark and dreariness of the putrefaction of a lost dream passing and a fallen Jerusalem behind him, eventually the angelic hand of mercy was extended by the Lord to him and a new dream given.

The tallness of the building is high as the tower of Babylon. By letting go of the old, we are prepared to grow into the new.

There is a traditional Mormon hymn called "Israel, Israel, God is Calling". The lyrics of the first verse are:

"Israel, Israel God is calling,
Calling thee from lands of woe,
Babylon the great is falling,
God shall her tow'rs o'er throw,
Come to Zion, come to Zion...

Israel, angels are descending,
From celestial worlds on high,
And to man their pow'r extending,
That the saints may homeward fly."

In Carthage, Illinois on the 27th of June in 1844 at about the 11th hour of the day (5:00 p.m.) on the second floor of the Carthage jail, Joseph Smith was shot by a mob.[34] He fell through the window and through the air to his death on the ground below, where his blood seeped into the pours of the earth; yet his spirit became free to homeward fly and ascend to his new life beyond the veil. It was reported by at least fifty-seven witnesses that on the 8th of August, 1844, while Joseph's successor, Brigham Young, spoke to those people that would soon build a temple, that he not only sounded like Joseph Smith, but appeared to be, as it were, Joseph himself. On that day the veil was thin and perhaps an angel descended to be with those he had served and loved, and to confirm to those to whom he had brought the legacy of Lehi of the reality of the Tree of Life.

---

[34] D&C 135:1

Conclusion

The harmony that can be found in the progress of the human family is not the result of the haphazard, the carefree and profane, but rather the symphonic opus magnum of Divine orchestration. The best words I can find to describe the metaphoric piece of the clay pot I've found are still yet limited. Furthermore, to keep that which is sacred in a safe place in our heart and mind ensures that the seeds of faith be not exposed to the fervent heat before they have taken root and found nurturance in our soul and so at times, not all that can be said should be said.

To be puffed up with pride associated with superfluous knowledge is indeed a lesser evil than to carry the spirit of contention. Yet, "knowledge does away with darkness, suspense and doubt; for these cannot exist where knowledge is". [35] Where light is, love may be secure. Where light and love are, life may sprout forth. May intuition and inspiration be upon us so that love might rise in our hearts and enlighten our minds...

> *...as we walk amongst oaks on a cold winter's eve,*
> *To walk amongst stars in spring to receive,*
> *To look toward the dawn, for the Sun to return,*
> *That the flame within, everlasting shall burn!*

---

[35] Stated by Joseph Smith Jr., extracted from "The Teachings of the Prophet Joseph Smith.", 1976, Deseret Book Co., p. 288.

Appendix A

Euler's Number and Chartres Labyrinth

The number of angels carrying golden vials in the concourses that surround the Savior in the Rose Window are 24. We may playfully note along the way here that 24 is related to 42 in a visually fun way. Applied to the labyrinth, we ask ourselves what may come of an exercise of letting go of the confinement of the physical units of the labyrinth in the physical plane and consider using mixed units that relate to metaphor. Let's check it out.

There is kind of a number riddle in the Chartres labyrinth if we consider the ratio of the circumference to the diameter using mixed units. 24 hours to 42 feet. The word 'feet' is found to have common etymological relationship with feather. The Sanskrit for the word feather is *patra*. And the European word *feather* comes from father. The Latin verb *patro* means 'to father'. Now let's look at the word "feet". Foot in Latin is *pede* or *pes*. In Spanish foot is *pie* which is also in the Spanish word *piedra*, which is equivalent to the Latin *petrae*. The ped, pet, pie and pat roots are also the basis for the word *path* as in footpath. The foot is a symbol of movement as is the feather. The Chartres labyrinth is laid out to be just that, a footpath. Hermes is often depicted as wearing sandals with wings. Hermes, like the two prophets that walk the streets of Jerusalem for 42 months, is a messenger. Hermes may move between worlds and is a god of transitions and boundaries; he is equivalent to the Egyptian god, Thoth. The ratio of the circumference of a circle and the diameter is surprisingly the ratio known as the transcendental number, *pi* which is very closely related to *pie*, or foot. The balance of the principles of Thoth and Ma'at may be expressed in riddle as 'hours', or Horus, as represented in the walk around the circumference of the labyrinth which is to be distinguished from walking the straight and undeviating course across the 42 foot diameter that is equated with the feathers or wings of Ma'at. The English word "hours" is an anagram of the name "Horus". Saying this in the prose of mathematical riddle, we might say 24 hours (Horus) to 42 feathers (Ma'at) is a 24/42 ratio. But funny enough the numbers 24 and 42 are mirror images of each other; or rather their digits are transposed similar to a mirror image. Gematria can be explored on the number sequence, 24 hours, 42 feet and 114 cogs and will be the number of that beast of the Mediterranean Isles, the Minotaur. I'll leave that to the reader to explore in favor of moving hastily to the more exciting main point.

What is exceptionally astounding and is the important result of this consideration, is that while the ratio of the circumference to the diameter yields the transcendental number π, in the case of the Chartres Cathedral, another transcendental number is found encoded in the labyrinth! If the number of cogs in the circumference of the labyrinth is used in ratio with the diameter, we find that the transcendental number e is encoded in the labyrinth! The ratio of the number of cogs to the diameter in feet is 114 cogs/42 feet = 2.71

This is absolutely astonishing! It is modernly believed that the first written use of the ratio is by Jacob Bernoulli, and that it wasn't until Leonhard Euler assigned the letter e to the ratio in 1736 in his work Mechanica, that e was formally designated as a transcendental number. However, the ratio is written in the Chartres labyrinth which was built in the 1200's A.D.!

Thusly, we may ask if Euler had any knowledge of the Chartres labyrinth. It turns out that he very likely did. Euler was fascinated with applying mathematics to mazes and theories of mapping as well as to the study of gears. His paper on the bridge of Konisberg Russia, "*Solutio problematis ad geometriam situs pertinensis*"[1], (Solution of a problem in the geometry of position), is considered to be the first paper on "graph theory". Furthermore, the ratio *e* was applied by Euler in his development of the "involute gear"[2]. It seems very likely then that Euler, thusly, would have encountered the use of the ratio, 2.71, in the Chartres labyrinth, which is, in fact, both a maze and a gear in appearance.

While it is astounding to discover this connectivity of the medieval architect to the modern scientist, it is yet further confounding to consider that the ratio may have been understood as early as 1260A.D. Perhaps it was used to model population growth? Were natural logarithms understood? It seems that this may be possible!

What we find to be even more astounding is that the aforementioned Phaistos disk contains 19 segments within the spiral and the spiral crosses the diameter 7 times. Taking this ratio of spiral segments to the number of times the spiral crosses the diameter, we get 19/7 or 2.71, which is again is Euler's number *e*! If that is not astounding enough, if we take the ratio of the number of segments in the circumference circle, excluding the entrance or "keystone", to the number of the times the spiral

---

[1] *Commentarii Academiae Scientarum Imperialis Petropolitanae*, (1736), 128–140 + Plate VIII

[2] Goss, Geoff *Application of analytical geometry to the form of gear teeth*, September 2013, Volume 18, Issue 9, pp 817–831

crosses a single radius we get 11/3.5 or 3.141285 which is the common approximation for π!

Photo Above: The Phaistos Disk Side A segments define the ratios for both π and Euler's number e as does the Chartres cathedral labyrinth! Photo courtesy of Heraklion Museum of Archaeology, Crete, Greece, through Wikimedia Commons per attribution 1.0 generic license terms 2/2015

Index